PRAYER &
SPIRITUAL
WARFARE

PRAYER & SPIRITUAL WARFARE

E. M. BOUNDS

WHITAKER
HOUSE

Publisher's note: This new edition from Whitaker House has been edited for the modern reader. Words, expressions, and sentence structure have been updated for clarity and readability.

Unless otherwise indicated, all Scripture quotations are taken from the King James Version of the Holy Bible. Scripture quotations marked (RV) are taken from the Revised Version of the Holy Bible.

PRAYER AND SPIRITUAL WARFARE

(previously published by Whitaker House under the title
The Necessity of Prayer)

ISBN: 0-88368-361-X
Printed in the United States of America
© 1984 by Whitaker House

Whitaker House
30 Hunt Valley Circle
New Kensington, PA 15068
www.whitakerhouse.com

Library of Congress Cataloging-in-Publication Data

Bounds, Edward M. (Edward McKendree), 1835–1913.
[Necessity of prayer]
Prayer and spiritual warfare / by E.M. Bounds.
p. cm.
Previously published under title: Necessity of prayer. Grand Rapids,
Mich. : Baker Book House, © 1991.
ISBN 0-88368-361-X (phk.)
1. Prayer—Christianity. I. Title.
BV210 .B576 2002
248.3'2—dc21
2002002243

3 4 5 6 7 8 9 10 11 12   **UI**   11 10 09 08 07 06 05 04

Contents

1
Prayer and Faith

A dear friend of mine who was quite a lover of the hunt, told me the following story. "Rising early one morning," he said, "I heard the barking of a number of dogs chasing deer. Looking at a large open field in front of me, I saw a young fawn making its way across the field and giving signs that its race was almost run. It leaped over the rails of the enclosed place and crouched within ten feet of where I stood. A moment later two of the hounds came over, and the fawn ran in my direction and pushed its head between my legs. I lifted the little thing to my breast, and, swinging round and round, fought off the dogs. Just then I felt that all the dogs in the West could not and would not capture that fawn after its weakness had appealed to my strength." So is it, when human helplessness appeals to Almighty God. I remember well, when the hounds of sin were after my soul, that at last I ran into the arms of Almighty God. —A. C. Dixon

Whenever a study of the principles of prayer is made, lessons concerning faith must accompany it. Faith is the essential quality in the heart of any man who desires to communicate with God. He must believe and stretch out his hands in faith for that which he cannot see or prove. Prayer is actually faith claiming and taking hold of its natural, immeasurable inheritance. True godliness is just as important in the realm of faith as it is in the area of prayer. Moreover, when faith ceases to pray, it ceases to live.

Faith does the impossible because it lets God undertake for us, and nothing is impossible with God. How great—without qualification or limitation—the power of faith is! If doubt can be banished from the heart and unbelief is made a stranger there, what we ask from God will surely come to pass. A believer has granted to him *"whatsoever he saith"* (Mark 11:23).

Prayer throws faith on God and God on the world. Only God can move mountains, but faith and prayer move God. In the cursing of the fig tree, our Lord demonstrated His power. (See Matthew 21:19–22.) Following that, He went on to say that large powers were committed to faith and prayer, not to kill but to make alive, not to blast but to bless.

At this point in our study, we need to emphasize some words of Jesus that are the very keystone of the arch of faith and prayer. The first is found in Mark 11:24: *"Therefore I say unto you, What things soever ye desire, when ye pray, believe that ye receive them, and ye shall have them."* We should think about that statement: *"Believe that ye receive them, and ye shall have them."* A faith that realizes, appropriates, and *takes* is described here. This faith is an awareness of God, an experienced communion, a real fact.

Is faith growing or declining as the years go by? Does faith stand strong and firm as sin abounds and the love of many grows cold? Does faith keep its hold as religion becomes a mere formality and worldliness becomes victorious? The question our Lord asked may appropriately be ours. *"When the Son of man cometh,"* He asked, *"shall he find faith on the earth?"* (Luke 18:8). We believe that He will, and it is our job today to see to it that the lamp of faith is trimmed and burning, until He returns.

Faith is the foundation of Christian character and the security of the soul. When Jesus was looking toward Peter's denial and cautioning him against it, He said to His disciple, *"Simon, Simon, behold, Satan hath desired to have you, that he may sift you as wheat: but I have prayed for thee, that thy faith fail not"* (Luke 22:31–32).

Our Lord was stating a central truth. It was Peter's faith He was seeking to guard. He knew that when faith breaks down, the foundations of spiritual life give way, and the entire structure of religious experience falls. It was Peter's faith that needed guarding. That is why Christ was concerned for the welfare of His disciple's soul and was determined to strengthen Peter's faith by His own victorious prayer.

Peter, in his second epistle, had this same idea in mind when he wrote of growing in grace as a measure of safety in the Christian life and as fruitfulness. *"And beside this,"* he declared, *"giving all diligence, add to your faith virtue; and to virtue knowledge; and to knowledge temperance; and to temperance patience; and to patience godliness"* (2 Pet. 1:5–6).

In this addition process, faith was the starting point, the basis of the other graces of the Spirit. Faith was the foundation on which other things were built. Peter did not urge his readers to add to works or gifts or virtues but to *faith.* In this business of growing in grace, much depends on starting right. There is a divine order. Peter was aware of it. He went on to say that we are to give constant care to making our calling and election secure (2 Pet. 1:10). This election is made sure by adding to faith that which is done by constant, earnest praying. Faith is kept alive by prayer. Every step in this adding of grace to grace is accompanied by prayer.

Faith that creates powerful praying is the faith that centers itself on a powerful Person. Faith in Christ's ability to *do* and to do *greatly* is the faith that prays greatly. In this way the leper laid hold of the power of Christ. *"Lord, if thou wilt,"* he cried, *"thou canst make me clean"* (Matt. 8:2). In this instance, we are shown how a faith centered in Christ's ability to *do* obtained the healing power.

It was concerning this very point that Jesus questioned the blind men who came to Him for healing: *"Believe ye that I am able to do this?"* He asked. *"They said unto Him, Yea, Lord. Then touched he their eyes, saying, According to your faith be it unto you"* (Matt. 9:28–29).

It was because He wanted to inspire faith in His ability to *do* that Jesus left behind Him that last, great statement, which, in the final analysis, is a ringing challenge to faith. *"All power,"* He declared, *"is given unto me in heaven and in earth"* (Matt. 28:18).

Again, faith is obedient. It goes when commanded, as did the nobleman who came to Jesus when his son was grievously sick. (See John 4:46–53.)

Likewise, such faith acts. Like the man who was born blind, it goes to wash in the pool of Siloam when *told* to wash. Like Peter on the Sea of Galilee, it instantly casts the net where Jesus commands, without question or doubt. Such faith promptly takes away the stone from the grave of Lazarus. A praying faith keeps the commandments of God and does those things that are pleasing in His sight. It asks, "Lord, what will you have me to do?" and answers quickly,

Prayer and Faith

"Speak, Lord, your servant hears." Obedience helps faith, and faith helps obedience. To do God's will is essential to true faith, and faith is necessary to absolute obedience.

Yet, faith is often called upon to wait patiently before God and is prepared for God's seeming delays in answering prayer. Faith does not grow disheartened because prayer is not immediately honored. It takes God at His Word and lets Him take what time He chooses in fulfilling His purposes and in carrying on His work. There are bound to be delays and long days of waiting for true faith, but faith accepts the conditions. It knows there will be delays in answering prayer and regards such delays as times of testing where it is privileged to show that it is made of courage and stern stuff.

The case of Lazarus was an instance where there was delay and where the faith of two good women was sorely tried. Lazarus was critically ill, and his sisters sent for Jesus. But, without any known reason, our Lord delayed going to the relief of His sick friend. The plea was urgent and touching: *"Lord, behold, he whom thou lovest is sick"* (John 11:3). But the Master was not moved by it, and the women's earnest request seemed to fall on deaf ears. What a trial of faith! Furthermore, our Lord's delay appeared to bring about hopeless disaster. While Jesus tarried, Lazarus died.

But the delay of Jesus was used in the interest of a greater good. Finally, He made His way to the home in Bethany.

> *Then said Jesus unto them plainly, Lazarus is dead. And I am glad for your sakes, that I was not there, to the intent ye may believe; nevertheless let us go unto him.* (John 11:14–15)

Prayer and Spiritual Warfare

Fear not, O tempted and tried believer. Jesus will come, if patience is exercised and faith holds fast. His delay will serve to make His coming more richly blessed. Pray on. Wait on. You cannot fail. If Christ delays, wait for Him. In His own good time, He will come and will not be late.

Delay is often the test and the strength of faith. How much patience is required when these times of testing come! Yet, faith gathers strength by waiting and praying. Patience has its perfect work in the school of delay. In some instances, delay is of the very nature of the prayer. God has to do many things before He gives the final answer. They are things that are essential to the lasting good of the person who is requesting the favor from Him.

Jacob prayed with purpose and eagerness to be delivered from Esau. But, before that prayer could be answered, there was much to be done with and for Jacob. He had to be changed as well as Esau. Jacob had to be made into a new man before Esau could be. Jacob had to be converted to God before Esau could be converted to Jacob.

Among the brilliant sayings of Jesus concerning prayer, none is more interesting than this:

> *Verily, verily, I say unto you, He that believeth on me, the works that I do shall he do also; and greater works than these shall he do; because I go unto my Father. And whatsoever ye shall ask in my name, that will I do, that the Father may be glorified in the Son. If ye shall ask any thing in my name, I will do it.*
>
> (John 14:12–14)

How wonderful these statements are of what God will do in answer to prayer! What great importance these ringing words have when prefaced with solemn truth! Faith in Christ is the basis of all working and all praying. All wonderful works depend on wonderful praying, and all praying is done in the name of Jesus Christ. The amazing, simple lesson is this praying in the name of the Lord Jesus! All other conditions are of little value. Everything else is given up except Jesus. The name of Christ—the person of our Lord and Savior Jesus Christ—must be supremely sovereign in the hour of prayer.

If Jesus dwells at the source of my life—if the flow of His life has replaced all of my life—then He can safely commit the praying to my will. If absolute obedience to Him is the inspiration and force of every movement of my life, then He will pledge Himself, by a duty as deep as His own nature, that whatever is asked will be granted. Nothing can be clearer, more distinct, more unlimited both in application and extent, than the plea and urgency of Christ: *"Have faith in God"* (Mark 11:22).

Faith covers worldly as well as spiritual needs. Faith scatters excessive anxiety and needless care about what will be eaten, what will be drunk, and what will be worn. Faith lives in the present and regards the day as being *"sufficient unto...the evil thereof"* (Matthew 6:34). It lives day by day and scatters all fears for tomorrow. Faith brings great peace of mind and perfect peace of heart.

> *Thou wilt keep him in perfect peace, whose mind is stayed on thee: because he trusteth in thee.*
>
> (Isa. 26:3)

When we pray, *"Give us this day our daily bread"* (Matt. 6:11), we are, in a measure, shutting tomorrow out of our prayer. We do not live for tomorrow, but for today. We do not look for tomorrow's grace or tomorrow's bread. Those who live in the present thrive best and get the most out of life. Those who pray best pray for today's, not tomorrow's, needs. Our prayer for tomorrow's needs may be unnecessary because they may not exist at all!

True prayers are born out of present trials and present needs. Bread for today is enough. Bread given for today is the strongest pledge that there will be bread tomorrow. Victory today is the assurance of victory tomorrow. Our prayers need to be focused on the present. We must trust God today and leave tomorrow entirely with Him. The present is ours; the future belongs to God. Prayer is the task and duty of each new day—daily prayer for daily needs.

As every day demands its bread, so every day demands its prayer. No amount of praying done today will be sufficient for tomorrow's praying. On the other hand, no praying for tomorrow is of any great value to us today. Today's manna is what we need; tomorrow God will see that our needs are supplied. This is the faith that God seeks to inspire.

So leave tomorrow, with its cares, needs, and troubles, in God's hands. There is no storing up of tomorrow's grace or tomorrow's praying. We cannot lay hold of today's grace to meet tomorrow's needs. We cannot have tomorrow's grace; we cannot eat tomorrow's bread; we cannot do tomorrow's praying. *"Sufficient unto the day is the evil thereof"* (Matt. 6:34). And, certainly, if we possess faith, sufficient also will be the good.

2
Prayer That Gets Results

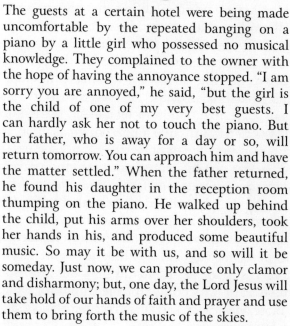

The guests at a certain hotel were being made uncomfortable by the repeated banging on a piano by a little girl who possessed no musical knowledge. They complained to the owner with the hope of having the annoyance stopped. "I am sorry you are annoyed," he said, "but the girl is the child of one of my very best guests. I can hardly ask her not to touch the piano. But her father, who is away for a day or so, will return tomorrow. You can approach him and have the matter settled." When the father returned, he found his daughter in the reception room thumping on the piano. He walked up behind the child, put his arms over her shoulders, took her hands in his, and produced some beautiful music. So may it be with us, and so will it be someday. Just now, we can produce only clamor and disharmony; but, one day, the Lord Jesus will take hold of our hands of faith and prayer and use them to bring forth the music of the skies.

—Anonymous

Genuine, authentic faith must be definite and free of doubt. It is not general in character or a mere belief in the being, goodness, and power of God. It is a faith that believes that the things that *"he saith shall come to pass"* (Mark 11:23). As faith is

15

specific, so the answer will also be definite. *"He shall have whatsoever he saith"* (Mark 11:23). Faith and prayer select the things, and God pledges Himself to do the very things that faith and persistent prayer name and ask Him to accomplish.

The Revised Version translates Mark 11:24 this way: *"All things whatsoever ye pray and ask for, believe that ye have received them, and ye shall have them."* Perfect faith always has in its keeping what perfect prayer asks for. How large and unqualified this area of operation is—all things whatsoever! How definite and specific the promise is—*"ye shall have them"*!

Our major concern is our faith—the problems of its growth and the actions of its strong development. A faith that holds on to the very things it asks for, without wavering, doubt, or fear—that is the faith we need. We need faith, like a pearl of great price, in the process and practice of prayer.

The above statement about faith and prayer is of supreme importance. *Faith must be definite and specific.* It must be an unqualified, unmistakable request for the things asked for. It should not be a vague, indefinite, shadowy thing. It must be something more than an ideal belief in God's willingness and ability to do something for us. It should be a definite, specific asking for and expectation of the things for which we ask. Note Mark 11:23: *"Whosoever…shall not doubt in his heart, but shall believe that those things which he saith shall come to pass; he shall have whatsoever he saith."*

Just as the faith and the request is definite, so the answer will be definite. The giving is not something other than the things prayed for, but the actual things sought and named. *"He shall have whatsoever he saith."* It is a certainty: *"he shall have."* The granting is unlimited both in quality and quantity.

Prayer That Gets Results

Faith and prayer select the subjects to be prayed for, thus determining what God is to do. *"He shall have whatsoever he saith."* Christ is ready to supply exactly and fully all the demands of faith and prayer. If the order to God is clear, specific, and definite, God will fill it exactly in agreement with the terms put before Him.

Faith is not an abstract belief in the Word of God or a mere mental belief. It is not a simple agreement of the understanding and will or a passive belief in facts, no matter how sacred or thorough. Faith is an operation of God, a divine illumination, a holy energy planted by the Word of God and the Spirit in the human soul. It is a spiritual, divine principle that takes from the supernatural and makes it an understandable thing by the faculties of time and sense.

Faith deals with God and is conscious of God. It deals with the Lord Jesus Christ and sees Him as a Savior. It deals with God's Word and lays hold of the truth. It deals with the Spirit of God and is energized and inspired by its holy fire. God is the great objective of faith, for faith rests its whole weight on His Word. Faith is not an aimless act of the soul, but a looking to God and a resting on His promises. Just as love and hope always have an objective, so also has faith. Faith is not believing just *anything*. It is believing God, resting in Him, and trusting His Word.

Faith gives birth to prayer. It grows stronger, strikes deeper, and rises higher in the struggles and wrestling of mighty petitioning. Faith is *"the substance of things hoped for"* (Hebrews 11:1), the confidence and reality of the inheritance of the saints. Faith, too, is humble and persistent. It can wait and pray. It can stay on its knees or lie in the dust. It is the one great condition of prayer. The lack of faith lies at the root of all poor, feeble, little, unanswered praying.

The nature and meaning of faith is proven more in what it does than by any definition it is given. So, if we turn to the record of faith given to us in that great honor roll in Hebrews 11, we see something of the wonderful results of faith.

What a glorious list it is of these men and women of faith! What marvelous achievements are recorded there and set to faith's credit! The inspired writer, exhausting his resources in cataloging the Old Testament saints who were such notable examples of wonderful faith, finally said,

> And what shall I more say? for the time would fail me to tell of Gedeon, and of Barak, and of Samson, and of Jephthae; of David also, and Samuel, and of the prophets. (Heb. 11:32)

Then the writer of Hebrews went on to tell of the unrecorded exploits brought about through the faith of the men of old, *"of whom the world was not worthy"* (v. 38). All these, he said, *"obtained a good report through faith"* (v. 39).

If we could only reproduce a race of saints with mighty faith and wonderful praying, what a glorious period of achievements would begin for the church and the world! The church does not need the intellectually great. The times do not demand wealthy men. People of great social influence are not what is required. Above everybody and everything else, the church and the whole wide world of humanity need men of faith and mighty prayer. We need men and women like the saints and heroes counted in Hebrews 11 who *"obtained a good report through faith."*

Prayer That Gets Results

Today, many men obtain a good report because of their monetary donations and their great mental gifts and talents. But there are few who obtain a good report because of their great faith in God or because of the wonderful things that come about through their great praying. Today, as much as at any time, we need men of great faith and men who are great in prayer. These are the two chief virtues that make men great in the eyes of God. These two things create conditions of real spiritual success in the life and work of the church. It is our main concern to see that we keep this kind of quality faith before God. This kind of faith grasps and holds in its keeping the things for which it asks without doubt and fear.

Doubt and fear are the twin enemies of faith. Sometimes they actually take the place of faith, and, although we pray, it is a restless, disquieted, uneasy, complaining prayer that we offer. Peter failed to walk on the waters of Galilee because he allowed the waves to break over him and swamp the power of his faith. Taking his eyes off the Lord and looking at the water around him, he began to sink and cry for help—"Lord, save me, or I perish!"

Doubts and fears should never be cherished or hidden. No one should cherish the false idea that he is a martyr to fear and doubt. It is of no credit to man's mental ability to cherish doubt of God. No comfort can possibly be gotten from such a thought. Our eyes should be taken off ourselves. They should be removed from our own weakness and allowed to rest totally on God's strength. *"Cast not away therefore your confidence, which hath great recompense of reward"* (Heb. 10:35). A simple, confiding faith, lived out day by day, will drive fear away. A faith that casts its burden on the Lord each hour of the day will drive away misgiving and deliver from doubt.

"Be careful for nothing; but in every thing by prayer and supplication with thanksgiving let your requests be made known unto God" (Phil. 4:6). That is the divine cure for all fear, anxiety, and excessive concern for the soul. All these are closely related to doubt and unbelief. This is the divine prescription for securing the peace that passes all understanding and keeps the heart and mind in quietness and peace.

All of us need to pay attention and heed the caution given in Hebrews 3:12: *"Take heed, brethren, lest there be in any of you an evil heart of unbelief, in departing from the living God."* We need to guard against unbelief as we would against an enemy. Faith needs to be cultivated. We need to keep on praying, *"Lord, increase our faith"* (Luke 17:5), for faith is capable of increasing. Paul's tribute to the Thessalonians was that their faith grew exceedingly. (See 2 Thessalonians 1:3.) Faith is increased by exercise, by being put to use. It is nourished by painful trials.

> That the trial of your faith, being much more precious than of gold that perisheth, though it be tried with fire, might be found unto praise and honour and glory at the appearing of Jesus Christ. (1 Pet. 1:7)

Faith grows by reading and meditating upon the Word of God. Most of all, faith thrives in an atmosphere of prayer.

It would be good if we stop and ask ourselves, Do I have faith in God; do I have *real* faith—faith that keeps me in perfect peace about the things of the earth and heaven? This is the most important question a man can propose and expect to be answered.

Prayer That Gets Results

And there is another question closely related to it in significance and importance: Do I really pray to God so that He hears me and answers my prayers; and do I truly pray to God so that I get directly from God the things I ask of Him?

It was said that Augustus Caesar found Rome a city of wood and left it a city of marble. The pastor who succeeds in changing his people from a prayerless to a prayerful people has done a greater work than Augustus did in changing a city from wood to marble. After all, this is the major work of the preacher. Primarily, he is dealing with prayerless people, of whom it is said, *"God is not in all* [their] *thoughts"* (Ps. 10:4).

The pastor meets such people everywhere all the time. His main business is to turn them from being forgetful about God, from lacking faith, from being prayerless, into people who habitually pray, believe in God, remember Him, and do His will. The preacher is not sent simply to persuade men to join the church or to get them to do better. He is sent to get them to pray, to trust God, and to keep God ever before their eyes so that they may not sin against Him.

The work of the ministry is to change unbelieving sinners into praying, believing saints. The call goes out by divine authority, *"Believe on the Lord Jesus Christ, and thou shalt be saved"* (Acts 16:31). We catch a glimpse of the tremendous importance of faith and the great value God has put on it when we remember that He has made it the one essential condition of being saved. *"For by grace are ye saved through faith"* (Eph. 2:8). So, when we think about the great importance of prayer, we find faith standing immediately by its side. By faith we are saved, and by faith we *stay* saved. Prayer introduces us to a life of faith. Paul

21

declared that the life he lived, he lived by faith in the Son of God, who loved him and gave Himself for him (Gal. 2:20)—that he walked by faith and not by sight (2 Cor. 5:7).

Prayer is absolutely dependent on faith. It has virtually no existence apart from it and accomplishes nothing unless it is faith's inseparable companion. Faith makes prayer effective and, in a certain important sense, must precede it. *"For he that cometh to God must believe that he is, and that he is a rewarder of them that diligently seek him"* (Heb. 11:6).

Before prayer ever starts toward God, before its petition is chosen and its requests made known, faith must have gone on ahead. It must have had its belief in the existence of God stated. It must have given its consent to the gracious truth that God is a rewarder of those who diligently seek His face.

This is the primary step in praying. In this regard, while faith does not bring the blessing, it puts prayer in a position to ask for it. It leads to another step of understanding by helping the petitioner believe that God is able and willing to bless.

Faith starts prayer working. It clears the way to the mercy seat. It gives assurance, first of all, that there is a mercy seat and that the High Priest waits there for us to come with our prayers. Faith opens the way for prayer to approach God. But it does more. Faith accompanies prayer with every step it takes. Faith is prayer's inseparable companion. When requests are made to God, faith turns the asking into obtaining. And faith follows prayer, since the spiritual life into which a believer is led by prayer is a life of faith. Faith, not a life of works, is the one prominent characteristic of the experience that believers are brought into through prayer.

Prayer That Gets Results

Faith makes prayer strong and gives it patience to wait on God. Faith believes that God is a rewarder. No truth is more clearly revealed and none is more encouraging in Scripture than this. Even the prayer closet has its promised reward: *"Thy Father which seeth in secret himself shall reward thee openly"* (Matt. 6:4). The most insignificant service given to a disciple in the name of the Lord surely receives its reward. Faith gives its hearty consent to this precious truth.

Yet, faith is narrowed down to one particular thing. It does not believe that God will reward everybody. It does not believe that He is a rewarder of all who pray, but that He is a rewarder of those who *"diligently seek him"* (Heb. 11:6). Faith rests its case on diligent prayer. It gives assurance and encouragement to diligent seekers after God, for it is they alone who are richly rewarded when they pray.

We constantly need to be reminded that faith is the one inseparable condition of successful praying. There are other conditions, but faith is the final, essential condition of true praying, as it is written: *"But without faith it is impossible to please him"* (v. 6).

James put this truth very plainly:

> *If any of you lack wisdom, let him ask of God, that giveth to all men liberally, and upbraideth not; and it shall be given him. But let him ask in faith, nothing wavering. For he that wavereth is like a wave of the sea driven with the wind and tossed. For let not that man think that he shall receive any thing of the Lord.*
> (James 1:5–7)

Doubting is always forbidden because it stands as an enemy to faith and hinders effective praying. Paul gave us a priceless truth relative to the conditions of successful praying. He said, *"I will therefore that men pray every where, lifting up holy hands, without wrath and doubting"* (1 Tim. 2:8).

All questioning must be guarded against and avoided. Fear and doubt have no place in true praying. Faith must assert itself and tell these enemies of prayer to depart.

Faith cannot be assigned too much authority, but prayer is the scepter that signals power. There is much spiritual wisdom in the following advice written by a famous saint:

> Do you want to be free from the bondage of corruption? Do you want to grow in grace in general and grow in grace in particular? If you do, your way is plain. Ask God for more faith. Beg Him morning, noon, and night, while you walk by the road, while you sit in the house, when you lie down, and when you rise up. Beg Him simply to impress divine things more deeply on your heart, to give you more and more of *"the substance of things hoped for"* and of *"the evidence of things not seen"* (Heb. 11:1).

Great incentives to pray are furnished in Scripture. Our Lord closed His teaching about prayer with the assurance and promise of heaven. The presence of Jesus Christ in heaven and the preparation He is making there for His saints help the weariness of praying. The assurance that He will come again to receive the saints strengthens and sweetens its difficult work! These things are the star of hope to prayer. They wipe away its tears and put the sweet odor of heaven into the bitterness of its cry. The spirit of a pilgrim makes praying easier. An earthbound, earth-satisfied spirit cannot pray. The flame of spiritual desire in such a heart has either gone out or is smoldering in a faint glow. The wings of its faith are clipped, its eyes are filmed, its tongue is silenced. But they who, in immovable faith and unceasing prayer, wait continually upon the Lord *do* renew their strength, *do* mount up with wings as eagles, *do* run and are not weary, *do* walk and not faint. (See Isaiah 40:31.)

3
Prayer and Trusting God

One evening I left my office in New York with a bitterly cold wind in my face. I had with me (as I thought) my thick, warm muffler, but when I proceeded to button up against the storm, I found that it was gone. I turned back, looked along the streets, searched my office, but in vain. I realized that I must have dropped it, and I prayed to God that I would find it; for such was the state of the weather that it would be running a great risk to proceed without it. I looked again up and down the surrounding streets, but without success. Suddenly, I saw a man on the opposite side of the road holding out something in his hand. I crossed over and asked him if that was my muffler. He handed it to me saying, "It was blown to me by the wind." He who rides upon the storm had used the wind as a means of answering prayer.
— William Horst

Prayer does not stand alone. It is not an isolated duty or an independent principle. It lives in fellowship with other Christian duties. It is married to other principles and is a partner with other graces. But prayer is firmly joined to faith. Faith gives it color and tone, shapes its character, and secures its results.

Prayer and Spiritual Warfare

Trust is faith that has become absolute, approved, and accomplished. When all is said and done, there is a sort of risk in faith and its exercise. But trust is firm belief; it is faith in full bloom. Trust is a conscious act, a fact of which we are aware. According to the scriptural concept, it is the eye of the newborn soul and the ear of the renewed soul. It is the feeling of the soul—the spiritual sight, hearing, taste, and touch. All these have to do with trust. How bright, distinct, conscious, powerful, and scriptural such a trust is! How different, feeble, dry, and cold are many forms of modern beliefs in comparison! These modern beliefs do not bring awareness of their presence. They do not bring *"joy unspeakable and full of glory"* (1 Pet. 1:8) from their exercise. They are, for the most part, adventures in the doubts of the soul. There is no safe, sure trust in anything. The whole transaction takes place in the area of *maybe* and *perhaps.*

Trust, like life, is feeling, though much more. An unfelt life is a contradiction. An unfelt trust is a misnaming and a false belief. Trust is the most felt of all qualities. It is *all* feeling, and it only works by love. An unfelt love is as impossible as an unfelt trust. The trust we are speaking about is a conviction. An unfelt conviction? How absurd!

Trust sees God doing things here and now. Yes, and more. It rises to a high place and looks into the invisible and the eternal. It realizes that God has done things and regards them as being already done. Trust brings eternity into the history and happenings of time. It transforms hope into the reality of fulfillment and changes promise into present possession. We know when we trust, just as we know when we see. We are conscious of our sense of touch. Trust sees, receives, holds. Trust is its own witness.

Prayer and Trusting God

Yet, quite often, faith is too weak to obtain God's greatest good immediately. It has to wait in loving, strong, prayerful, pressing obedience until it grows in strength and is able to bring down the eternal into the areas of experience and time.

Up to this point, trust shapes all its forces. Here it holds. In the struggle, trust's grasp becomes mightier, and it grasps for itself all that God has done for it in His eternal wisdom and fullness of grace.

In the matter of waiting in mighty prayer, faith rises to its highest level and becomes the gift of God. It becomes the blessed character and expression of the soul that is secured by a constant fellowship with and tireless request to God.

Jesus Christ clearly taught that faith was the condition on which prayer was answered. When our Lord cursed the fig tree, the disciples were very surprised that its withering had actually taken place. Their remarks indicated their unbelief. It was then that Jesus said to them:

> *Have faith in God. For verily I say unto you, That whosoever shall say unto this mountain, Be thou removed, and be thou cast into the sea; and shall not doubt in his heart, but shall believe that those things which he saith shall come to pass; he shall have whatsoever he saith. Therefore I say unto you, What things soever ye desire, when ye pray, believe that ye receive them, and ye shall have them.* (Mark 11:22–24)

There is no place where trust grows so readily and richly as in the prayer closet. Its unfolding and development are rapid and wholesome when they are kept regularly and well. When these appointments are sincere, full, and free, trust grows increasingly. The eye and presence of God give active life to trust, just like the eye and presence of the sun make fruit and flower grow and all things glad and bright with fuller life.

Faith and trust in the Lord form the keynote and foundation of prayer. Primarily, it is not trust in the Word of God but rather trust in the person of God, for trust in the person of God must precede trust in the Word of God. *"Ye believe in God, believe also in me"* (John 14:1) is the demand our Lord makes on the personal trust of His disciples. The person of Jesus Christ must be central to the eye of trust. Jesus sought to impress this great truth on Martha when her brother lay dead in their home at Bethany. Martha stated her belief in the resurrection of her brother: *"Martha saith unto him, I know that he shall rise again in the resurrection at the last day"* (John 11:24).

Jesus lifted her trust above the mere fact of the resurrection, to His own person, by saying,

> *I am the resurrection, and the life: he that believeth in me, though he were dead, yet shall he live: and whosoever liveth and believeth in me shall never die. Believest thou this? She saith unto him, Yea, Lord: I believe that thou art the Christ, the Son of God, which should come into the world.* (John 11:25–27)

Trust in a historical fact or a mere record may be a very passive thing, but trust in a person strengthens the quality. It bears fruit and supplies it with love. The trust that supplies prayer centers in a Person.

Trust goes even further than this. The trust that inspires our prayer must not only be one in the person of God, and of Christ, but also in their ability and willingness to grant the thing prayed for. It is not only, *"Trust in the LORD"* (Ps. 37:3), but also, *"for in the LORD JEHOVAH is everlasting strength"* (Isa. 26:4).

Prayer and Trusting God

The trust that our Lord taught as a condition of effective prayer is not from the head but from the heart. It is trust that does not doubt. Such trust has the divine assurance that it will be honored with large and satisfying answers. The strong promise of our Lord brings faith down to the present and counts on a present answer.

Do we believe without a doubt? When we pray, do we believe that we will receive the things we ask for, not on a future day, but then and there? This is the teaching of this inspiring Scripture. How we need to pray, *"Lord, increase our faith"* (Luke 17:5) until doubt is gone and absolute trust claims the promised blessings as its very own.

This is no easy condition. It is only reached after many failures, much praying, many wailings, and much trial of faith. May our faith increase until we realize and receive all the fullness that there is in the name of Jesus, which guarantees to do so much.

Our Lord puts forth trust as the very foundation of praying. The background of prayer is trust. The whole purpose of Christ's ministry and work was dependent on absolute trust in His Father. The center of trust is God. Mountains of difficulties and all other hindrances to prayer are moved out of the way by trust and its strong follower, faith.

When trust is perfect and there is no doubt, prayer is simply the outstretched hand ready to receive. Trust perfected is prayer perfected. Trust looks to receive the thing asked for and gets it. Trust is not a belief that God *can* bless or that He *will* bless, but that He *does* bless, here and now. Trust always operates in the present tense. Hope looks toward the future. Trust looks to the present. Hope expects. Trust possesses. Trust receives what prayer acquires. So, what prayer needs, at all times, is abiding and abundant trust.

The disciples' unfortunate lack of trust and resulting failure to do what they were sent out to do is seen in the case of the lunatic son. His father brought him to nine of them while their Master was on the Mount of Transfiguration. The boy, sadly tormented, was brought to these men to be cured of his sickness. They had been commissioned to do this very kind of work. This was part of their mission. They tried to cast the demon from the boy but noticeably failed. The demon was too much for them. They were humiliated at their failure while their enemies were victorious.

During the incident, Jesus drew near. He was informed of the circumstances and conditions connected with it. Here is the account of what followed:

> *Then Jesus answered and said, O faithless and perverse generation, how long shall I be with you? how long shall I suffer you? bring him hither to me. And Jesus rebuked the devil; and he departed out of him: and the child was cured from that very hour. Then came the disciples to Jesus apart, and said, Why could not we cast him out?...Howbeit this kind goeth not out but by prayer and fasting.*
>
> (Matt. 17:17–19, 21)

Where was the difficulty of these men? They had been careless in cultivating their faith by prayer, and, as a result, their trust utterly failed. They did not trust God, Christ, or the authenticity of His mission or their own. It has been the same since, in many a crisis in the church of God. Failure has resulted from a lack of trust, a weakness of faith, and a lack of prayerfulness. Many failures in revival efforts have been traceable to the same cause. Faith has not been nurtured and made powerful by prayer. Neglect of the inner chamber is the solution of most spiritual failure. This is also true of our personal struggles with Satan when we attempt to cast out demons. Being on our knees in private fellowship with God is our only assurance that we will have Him with us in our personal struggles or in our efforts to convert sinners.

When people came to Him, our Lord put their trust in Him and the divinity of His mission in the forefront. He did not give a definition of trust. He did not furnish a theological discussion or analysis of it. He knew that men would see what faith was by what faith *did*. They would see from its free exercise that trust grew up, automatically, in His presence. It was the product of His work, His power, and His person. These furnished and created a favorable atmosphere for its exercise and development. Trust is altogether too simple for verbal definition. It is too sincere and spontaneous for theological terms. The very simplicity of trust is what staggers many people. They look for some great thing to come to pass, while all the time *"the word is nigh thee, even in thy mouth, and in thy heart"* (Rom. 10:8).

When the sad news of his daughter's death was brought to Jairus, our Lord interrupted saying, *"Fear not: believe only, and she shall be made whole"* (Luke 8:50). To the woman with the issue of blood, who stood trembling before Him, He said, *"Daughter, be of good comfort: thy faith hath made thee whole; go in peace"* (v. 48).

As the two blind men followed Him, pressing their way into the house, He said, *"According to your faith be it unto you. And their eyes were opened"* (Matt. 9:29–30). When the paralytic was let down by four of his friends through the roof of the house where Jesus was teaching and placed before Him, it is recorded: *"And Jesus seeing their faith said unto the sick of the palsy; Son, be of good cheer; thy sins be forgiven thee"* (Matt. 9:2).

When Jesus dismissed the centurion whose servant was seriously ill, He did it in a particular manner. The centurion had come to Jesus with the prayer that He speak the healing word without even going to his house. Jesus did the following: *"And Jesus said unto the centurion, Go thy way; and as thou hast believed, so be it done unto thee. And his servant was healed in the selfsame hour"* (Matt. 8:13). When the poor leper fell at Jesus' feet and cried out for relief saying, *"Lord, if thou wilt, thou canst make me clean"* (v. 2), Jesus immediately granted his request, and the man glorified Him with a loud voice.

The Syrophenician woman came to Jesus about her troubled daughter. Making the case her own, she prayed, *"Lord, help me"* (Matt. 15:25). Jesus honored her faith and prayer, saying, *"O woman, great is thy faith: be it unto thee even as thou wilt. And her daughter was made whole from that very hour"* (v. 28).

After the disciples had utterly failed to cast the demon out of the epileptic boy, the father of the boy came to Jesus with a sad, despairing cry, *"If thou canst do any thing, have compassion on us, and help us"* (Mark 9:22). But Jesus replied, *"If thou canst believe, all things are possible to him that believeth"* (v. 23).

Blind Bartimaeus, sitting by the wayside, heard our Lord as He passed by and cried out pitifully, *"Jesus, thou son of David, have mercy on me"* (Mark 10:47). The keen ears of our Lord immediately caught the sound of prayer. He said to the beggar, *"Go thy way; thy faith hath made thee whole. And immediately he received his sight, and followed Jesus in the way"* (v. 52).

Prayer and Trusting God

Jesus spoke cheerful, soul-comforting words to the weeping, penitent woman who washed His feet with her tears and wiped them with her hair: *"Thy faith hath saved thee; go in peace"* (Luke 7:50).

One day Jesus healed ten lepers at one time, in answer to their united prayer, *"Jesus, Master, have mercy on us"* (Luke 17:13). He told them to go and show themselves to the priests. *"And it came to pass, that, as they went, they were cleansed"* (v. 14).

4
Prayer and Desire

There are those who will mock me and tell me to stick to my trade as a cobbler. They will tell me to not trouble my mind with philosophy and theology. But the truth of God did so burn in my bones that I took my pen in hand and began to set down what I had seen. —Jacob Behmen

Desire is not merely a simple wish. It is a deep-seated desire and an intense longing for accomplishment. In the realm of spiritual affairs, it is an important addition to prayer. It is so important that one could almost say desire is an absolute essential of prayer. Desire precedes and accompanies prayer. Desire goes before prayer and is created and intensified by it. Prayer is the oral expression of desire. If prayer is asking God for something, then prayer must be expressed. Prayer comes out into the open. Desire is silent. Prayer is heard. The deeper the desire, the stronger the prayer. Without desire, prayer is a meaningless mumble of words. Such uninterested, formal praying, with no heart, feeling, or real desire accompanying it, is to be avoided like a plague. Its exercise is a waste of precious time, and no real blessing results from it.

Prayer and Spiritual Warfare

Yet, even if it is discovered that desire is honestly absent, we should pray anyway. We ought to pray. The *ought* comes in, in order for desire and expression to be produced. God's Word commands it. Our judgment tells us we ought to pray—whether we feel like it or not—and not allow our feelings to determine our prayer habits. In such circumstances, we ought to pray for the *desire* to pray. This desire is God-given and heaven-born. We should pray for desire. Then, when desire has been given, we should pray according to its principles. The lack of spiritual desire should grieve us and lead us to mourn its absence. We should earnestly seek for its prize so that our praying would be an expression of "the soul's sincere desire."

A sense of need creates, or should create, earnest desire. The stronger the need before God, the greater the desire and the more earnest the prayer should be. The *"poor in spirit"* (Matt. 5:3) are highly competent to pray.

Hunger is an active sense of physical need. It prompts the request for food. In like manner, the inward awareness of spiritual need creates desire, and desire creates prayer. Desire is an inward longing for something that we do not possess and need. It is something that God has promised and that can be secured by earnest prayer at His throne of grace.

Spiritual desire, carried to a higher degree, is the evidence of the new birth. It is born in the renewed soul: *"As newborn babes, desire the sincere milk of the word, that ye may grow thereby"* (1 Pet. 2:2).

The absence of this holy desire in the heart is proof that there has been a decline in spiritual joy or that the new birth has never taken place. *"Blessed are they which do hunger and thirst after righteousness: for they shall be filled"* (Matt. 5:6).

Prayer and Desire

These heaven-given appetites are proof of a renewed heart and the evidence of a stirring spiritual life. Physical appetites are the characteristics of a living body, not a corpse. Spiritual desires belong to a soul made alive to God. As the renewed soul hungers and thirsts after righteousness, these holy, inward desires break out into earnest, petitioning prayer.

In prayer we are dependent on the name and power of Jesus Christ, our great High Priest. Searching the accompanying conditions and forces in prayer, we find its vital basis, which is seated in the human heart. It is not simply our need; it is the heart's desire for what we need and for what we feel urged to pray about. *Desire is the will in action.* It is a strong, conscious longing that is excited in the inner man for some great good. Desire exalts the object of its longing and sets the mind on it. It has choice, attitude, and fire in it. Prayer, based on these, is genuine and specific. It knows its need, feels and sees the thing that will meet it, and hurries to acquire it.

Holy desire is helped by devout study. Meditation on our spiritual need and on God's readiness and ability to correct it helps desire to grow. Serious thought practiced before praying increases desire. It makes prayer more insistent and tends to save us from the danger of private prayer—wandering thought. We fail much more in desire than in its outward expression. We keep the form while the inner life fades and almost dies.

One might ask whether the feebleness of our desire for God the Father, the Holy Spirit, and all the fullness of Christ is the cause of our lack of prayer. Do we really feel this inward hunger and desire for heavenly treasures? Do the inborn groanings of desire stir our souls to mighty wrestlings? Oh, the fire burns entirely too low. The flaming heat of the soul has been toned down to a lukewarmness. This, we should remember, was the major cause of the sad, desperate condition of the Laodicean Christians. Because of this condition, the awful condemnation is written about them: "[You are] *rich, and increased with goods, and* **have need of nothing;** *and knowest not that thou art wretched, and miserable, and poor, and blind, and naked"* (Rev. 3:17, emphasis added).

Again, we might ask, do we have that desire that presses us into close communion with God? Do we have the desire that is filled with silent pain that keeps us there through the agony of an intense, soul-stirred prayer? Our hearts need to be worked over, not only to get the evil out of them, but to get the good into them. They need to be worked over so that the foundation and inspiration to the incoming good is strong, moving desire. This holy, fervent flame in the soul awakens the interest of heaven, attracts God's attention, and places the inexhaustible riches of divine grace at the disposal of those who exercise it.

The dampening of the flame of holy desire is destructive to the vital, aggressive forces in church life. God expects to be represented by a fiery church or He is not, in any proper sense, represented at all. God Himself is all fire, and His church, if it is to be like Him, must also be like white heat. The only things that His church can afford to be on fire about are the great, eternal interests of heaven-born, God-given faith.

Yet, holy desire does not have to be fussy in order to be consuming. Our Lord was the incarnate opposite of nervous excitability, the absolute opposite of intolerant or noisy speech. Still, the zeal of God's house consumed Him. And the world is still feeling the glow of His fierce, consuming flame. They are responding to it with an ever increasing readiness and an even larger response.

A lack of passion in prayer is a sure sign of the lack of depth and the intensity of desire. The absence of intense desire is a sure sign of God's absence from the heart! To reduce fervor is to retire from God. He can and does tolerate in His children many things in the areas of weakness and mistakes. He can and will pardon sin when the repentant one prays.

But two things are intolerable to Him—insincerity and lukewarmness. Lack of heart and heat are two things He hates. He said to the Laodiceans, in unmistakable severity and condemnation: *"I would thou wert cold or hot. So then because thou art lukewarm, and neither cold nor hot, I will spue thee out of my mouth"* (Rev. 3:15–16).

This was God's precise judgment on the lack of fire in one of the seven churches. It is His accusation against individual Christians for the fatal lack of sacred zeal. Fire is the motivating power in prayer. Religious principles that do not come out of fire have neither force nor effect. Fire is the wing on which faith ascends. Passion is the soul of prayer. It is the *"effectual fervent prayer of a righteous man* [that] *availeth much"* (James 5:16). Love is kindled in a flame, and zeal is its life. Flame is the air that true Christian experience breathes. It feeds on fire. It can withstand anything except a weak flame. It dies, chilled and starved.

True prayer *must* be aflame. The Christian life and character need to be on fire. Lack of spiritual heat creates more unbelief than lack of faith does. If man is not wholly interested in the things of heaven, he is not interested in them at all. The fiery souls are those who conquer in the day of battle. They are those from whom the kingdom of heaven suffers violence and who take it by force (Matt. 11:12). The stronghold of God is taken only by those who storm it in worshipful earnestness and besiege it with fiery, unshakeable zeal.

Nothing short of being red-hot for God can keep the glow of heaven in our hearts during these chilly days. The early Methodists had no heating in their churches. They said that the flame in the pew and the fire in the pulpit must be sufficient to keep them warm. And we, today, need to have the live coal from God's altar and the consuming flame from heaven glowing in our hearts. This flame is not mental power or fleshly energy. It is divine, intense, dross-consuming fire in the soul. It is the very being of the Spirit of God.

No scholarship, pure speech, breadth of mental outlook, fluent language, or elegance can make up for the lack of fire. Prayer ascends by fire. Flame gives prayer access as well as wings. It gives prayer acceptance as well as energy. There is no incense without fire, no prayer without flame.

Ardent desire is the basis of unceasing prayer. It is not a shallow, fickle tendency, but a strong yearning—an unquenchable desire that permeates, glows, burns, and fixes the heart. It is the flame of a present and active principle ascending up to God. It is ardor propelled by desire that burns its way to the throne of mercy and gets its request. It is the determination of desire that gives victory in a great struggle of prayer. It is the burden of a weighty desire that sobers, makes restless, and reduces to quietness the soul just emerged from its mighty wrestlings. It is the inclusive character of desire that arms prayer with a thousand requests. It clothes it with an indestructible courage and an all-conquering power.

Prayer and Desire

The Syrophenician woman is an object lesson of desire. The demanding widow represents desire gaining its end, overcoming obstacles that would be insurmountable to weaker instincts.

Prayer is not the rehearsal of a mere performance. It is not an indefinite, widespread demand. Desire, while it ignites the soul, holds it to the object sought. Prayer is a necessary phase of spiritual habit, but it ceases to be prayer when it is carried on by habit alone. Depth and strength of spiritual desire give intensity and depth to prayer. The soul cannot be unconcerned when some great desire heats and inflames it. The urgency of our desire holds us to the thing desired with a courage that refuses to be lessened or loosened. It stays, pleads, persists, and refuses to let go until the blessing has been given.

> Lord, I cannot let Thee go,
> Till a blessing Thou bestow;
> Do not turn away Thy face;
> Mine's an urgent, pressing case.

The secret of cowardice, the lack of demanding, and the scarcity of courage and strength in prayer lie in the weakness of spiritual desire. The failure of prayer is the fearful evidence of that desire having ceased to live. That soul whose desire for Him no longer pushes into the inner room, has turned from God. There is no successful prayer without consuming desire. Of course, there can be much *seeming* to pray, without desire of any kind.

Many things may be listed and much ground covered. But does desire make up the list? Does desire map out the region to be covered? The answer hangs on the issue of whether our petitioning is babbling or prayer.

Prayer and Spiritual Warfare

Desire is intense but narrow. It cannot spread itself over a wide area. It wants a few things and wants them badly. It wants them so badly that nothing but God's willingness to answer can bring it ease or contentment.

Desire shoots at its objective. There may be many things that are desired, but they are specifically and individually felt and expressed. David did not yearn for everything. He did not allow his desires to spread out everywhere and hit nothing. Here is the way his desires ran and found expression:

> One thing have I desired of the LORD, that will I seek after; that I may dwell in the house of the LORD all the days of my life, to behold the beauty of the LORD, and to inquire in His temple. (Ps. 27:4)

It is this singleness of desire, this definite yearning, that counts in praying and drives prayer directly to the core and center of supply.

In the Beatitudes, Jesus voiced the words that bear directly upon the inborn desires of a renewed soul with the promise that they will be granted. *"Blessed are they which do hunger and thirst after righteousness: for they shall be filled"* (Matt. 5:6).

This, then, is the basis of prayer that expects an answer. It is that strong, inward desire that has entered the spiritual appetite and demands to be satisfied. For us, it is entirely true and frequent that our prayers operate in the dry area of a mere wish or in the lifeless area of a memorized prayer. Sometimes our prayers are merely stereotyped expressions of set phrases and standardized dimensions. The freshness and life has gone out long ago.

Without desire, there is no burden of the soul, no sense of need, no enthusiasm, no vision, no strength,

Prayer and Desire

and no glow of faith. There is no strong pressure, no holding on to God with a deathless, despairing grasp—*"I will not let thee go, except thou bless me"* (Gen. 32:26). There is no total surrender as there was with Moses. Lost in the agony of a desperate, stubborn, and all-consuming request, he cried, *"Yet now, if thou wilt forgive their sin—; and if not, blot me, I pray thee, out of thy book which thou hast written"* (Exod. 32:32). Or, there was also John Knox when he pleaded, "Give me Scotland, or may I die!"

God draws very close to the praying soul. To see God, know God, and live for God—these form the objective of all true praying. So, praying is, after all, inspired to seek after God. Prayer desire is ignited to see God and have a clearer, fuller, sweeter, and richer revelation of God. To those who pray this way, the Bible becomes a new Bible and Christ a new Savior by the light and revelation of the prayer closet.

We affirm and reaffirm that burning desire because the best and most powerful gifts and graces of the Spirit of God are the real heritage of true praying. Self and service cannot be divorced. They cannot possibly be separated. More than that, desire must be made intensely personal. It must be centered on God with an insatiable hungering and thirsting after Him and His righteousness. *"My soul thirsteth for God, for the living God"* (Ps. 42:2). The essential prerequisite for all true praying is a deep-seated desire that seeks after God Himself. It remains unsatisfied until the choice gifts in heaven have been richly and abundantly given.

5
Prayer and Enthusiasm

———— •·❦·• ————

St. Teresa rose off her deathbed to finish her work. She inspected, with all her quickness of eye and love of order, the whole house where she had been carried to die. She saw everything put in its proper place and everyone answering to their proper order. After that she attended to the divine offices of the day. Then she went back to her bed, summoned her daughter around her...and, with David's penitential prayers on her tongue, Teresa of Avila went forth to meet her Bridegroom.
—Alexander Whyte

P rayer without burning enthusiasm stakes nothing on the issue, because it has nothing to stake. It comes with empty hands. These hands are listless, empty, and have never learned the lesson of clinging to the cross.

Prayer without enthusiasm has no heart in it. It is an empty thing, an unfit vessel. Heart, soul, and life must find a place in all real praying. Heaven must be made to feel the force of this crying unto God.

Paul was a notable example of the man who possesses a fervent spirit of prayer. His petitioning was all-consuming. It centered immovably upon the object of his desire and the God who was able to meet it.

Prayer and Spiritual Warfare

Prayers must be red-hot. It is the fervent prayer that is effective and profitable. Coldness of spirit hinders praying. It takes fire to make prayers go. A warm soul creates a favorable atmosphere to prayer because it is favorable to fervency. Prayer ascends to heaven by fire. Yet, fire is not fuss, heat, or noise. Heat is intensity—something that glows and burns.

God wants warmhearted servants. The Holy Spirit comes *as a fire* to dwell in us. We are to be baptized with the Holy Spirit and with fire. (See Luke 3:16.) Fervency is warmth of soul. A phlegmatic temperament is detestable to vital experience. If our faith does not set us on fire, it is because we have frozen hearts. God dwells in a flame; the Holy Spirit descends in fire. To be absorbed in God's will and to be so in earnest about doing it that our whole being takes fire are the qualifying conditions of the man who would engage in effective prayer.

Our Lord warns us against feeble praying. *"Men ought always to pray, and not to faint"* (Luke 18:1), said Christ to His disciples. This means that we are to possess enough enthusiasm to carry us through the severe and long periods of pleading prayer. Fire makes one alert, vigilant, and brings him out more than a conqueror. The atmosphere about us is too heavily charged with resisting forces for limp and languid prayers to make headway. It takes heat, fervency, and meteoric fire to push through to the upper heavens where God dwells with His saints in light.

Many of the great Bible characters were notable examples of fervency of spirit when they were seeking God. The psalmist declared with great earnestness, *"My soul breaketh for the longing that it hath unto thy judgments at all times"* (Ps. 119:20). What strong heart desires are here! What earnest soul longings there are

Prayer and Enthusiasm

for the Word of the living God! An even greater fervency is expressed by him in another place:

> As the hart panteth after the water brooks, so panteth my soul after thee, O God. My soul thirsteth for God, for the living God: when shall I come and appear before God? (Ps. 42:1–2)

This is the word of a man who lived in a state of grace and had been deeply and supernaturally fulfilled in his soul.

Fervency before God counts in the hour of prayer and finds a speedy and rich reward at His hands. The psalmist gave us this statement of what God had done for the king, as his heart turned toward his Lord: *"Thou hast given him his heart's desire, and hast not withholden the request of his lips"* (Ps. 21:2).

At another time, he expressed himself directly to God in making his request: *"Lord, all my desire is before thee; and my groaning is not hid from thee"* (Ps. 38:9). What a cheerful thought! Our inward groanings, our secret desires, our heart longings are not hidden from the eyes of Him with whom we deal in prayer.

The incentive to fervency of spirit before God is precisely the same as it is for continued and earnest prayer. While fervency is not prayer, yet it comes out of an earnest soul and is precious in the sight of God. Fervency in prayer is the forerunner of what God will do by way of an answer. When we seek His face in prayer, God stands pledged to give us the desire of our hearts in proportion to the fervency of spirit we exhibit.

Fervency has its seat in the heart, not in the brain or intellectual faculties of the mind. Fervency, therefore, is not an expression of the intellect. Fervency of spirit is something far above poetical fancy or sentimental imagery. It is something besides preference, which contrasts likes with dislikes. Fervency is the pulse and movement of the emotional nature.

It is not our job to create fervency of spirit at will, but we can ask God to implant it. Then, it is ours to nourish and cherish, guard against extinction, and prevent its lessening or decline. The process of personal salvation is not just to pray and express our desires to God. But it is to acquire a fervent spirit and seek to cultivate it. It is never wrong to ask God to create in us and keep alive the spirit of fervent prayer.

Fervency has to do with God, just as prayer has to do with Him. Desire always has an objective. If we desire at all, we desire *something*. The degree of enthusiasm with which we form our spiritual desires will always serve to determine the earnestness of our praying. In this relation, Adoniram Judson has said,

> A travailing spirit, the throes of a great burdened desire, belongs to prayer. A fervency strong enough to drive away sleep, which devotes and inflames the spirit and which retires all earthly ties, all this belongs to wrestling, prevailing prayer. The Spirit, the power, the air, and food of prayer is in such a spirit.

Prayer must be clothed with fervency, strength, and power. It is the force that, centered on God, determines the amount of Himself given out for earthly good. Men who are fervent in spirit are bent on attaining righteousness, truth, grace, and all other sublime, powerful graces that adorn the character of the authentic, unquestioned child of God.

Prayer and Enthusiasm

God once declared the following message by the mouth of the prophet Hanani to Asa. Asa, at one time, had been true to God. But, through success and material prosperity, he lost his faith.

> *The eyes of the LORD run to and fro throughout the whole earth, to show himself strong in the behalf of them whose heart is perfect toward him. Herein thou hast done foolishly: therefore from henceforth thou shalt have wars.* (2 Chron. 16:9)

God had heard Asa's prayer in early life; but because he had given up the life of prayer and simple faith, disaster and trouble came to him.

In Romans 15:30 we have the word *strive* in the request that Paul made for prayerful cooperation. In Colossians 4:12 we have the same word, but translated differently: *"Epaphras...always labouring fervently for you in prayers."* Paul charged the Romans to strive together with him in prayer, that is, to help him with his struggle in prayer. The word *strive* means "to enter into a contest, to fight against adversaries." It also means "to engage with fervent zeal to endeavor to obtain."

These recorded instances of the exercise and reward of faith allow us to see that, in almost every instance, faith was blended with trust until the former was swallowed up in the latter. It is hard to properly distinguish the specific activities of these two qualities, faith and trust. But there is a point at which faith is relieved of its burden, so to speak, and trust comes along and says, "You have done your part. The rest is mine!"

In the incident of the barren fig tree, our Lord transfers the marvelous power of faith to His disciples.

Prayer and Spiritual Warfare

To their exclamation, *"How soon is the fig tree withered away!"* (Matt. 21:20), He said,

> *If ye have faith, and doubt not, ye shall not only do this which is done to the fig tree, but also if ye shall say unto this mountain, Be thou removed, and be thou cast into the sea; it shall be done. And all things, whatsoever ye shall ask in prayer, believing, ye shall receive.* (Matt. 21:21–22)

When a believer achieves these magnificent proportions of faith, he steps into the realm of absolute trust. He stands without a tremor at the height of his spiritual outreaching. He has attained faith's top step, which is unswerving, unalterable, unquestionable trust in the power of the living God.

6
Prayer That Is Persistent

———•·❦❧·•———

How glibly we talk of praying without ceasing! Yet, we are quite ready to quit if our prayer remains unanswered but one week or month! We assume that by a stroke of His arm or an action of His will, God will give us what we ask. It never seems to dawn on us that He is the Master of nature, as of grace, and that sometimes He chooses one way, and sometimes another, to do His work. It takes years, sometimes, to answer a prayer. When it is answered, we can look back to see that it did take years. But God knows all the time. It is His will that we pray and pray and still pray, and so come to know indeed what it is to pray without ceasing.   —Anonymous

Our Lord Jesus declared that *"men ought always to pray, and not to faint"* (Luke 18:1). The parable that comes after these words was taught with the intention of saving men from faintheartedness and weakness in prayer. Our Lord wanted to teach us to guard against negligence and to encourage and bring about persistence. We cannot have two opinions regarding the importance of the exercise of this indispensable quality in our praying.

53

Prayer and Spiritual Warfare

Persistent prayer is a mighty move of the soul toward God. It is a stirring of the deepest forces of the soul toward the throne of heavenly grace. It is the ability to hold on, press on, and wait. Restless desire, restful patience, and strength to hold on are all embraced in it. It is not an incident or a performance, but a passion of soul. It is not something half-needed, but a sheer necessity.

The wrestling quality in persistent prayer does not spring from physical violence or fleshly energy. It is not an impulse of energy or a mere earnestness of the soul. It is an inward force or ability planted and roused by the Holy Spirit. Virtually, it is the intercession of the Spirit of God in us. It is *the effectual fervent prayer...*[that] *availeth much"* (James 5:16). The divine Spirit supplies every part of us with the energy of His own striving. This is the essence of the persistence that urges our praying at the mercy seat to continue until the fire falls and the blessing descends. This wrestling in prayer is not loud or vehement, but quiet, firm, and urgent. When there are no visible outlets for its mighty forces, it may be silent.

Nothing distinguishes the children of God so clearly and strongly as prayer. It is the one infallible mark and test of being a Christian. Christian people are prayerful. The worldly-minded are prayerless. Christians call on God. The world ignores God and does not call on His name. But even the Christian has to cultivate *continual* prayer. It must be habitual, but it must be much more than a habit. It is duty, yet it is one that rises far above and goes beyond the ordinary implications of the term. It is the expression of a relationship with God, a yearning for divine communion. It is the outward and upward flow of the inner life toward its original fountain. It is a statement of the soul's origin, a claiming of sonship that links man to the eternal.

Prayer has everything to do with molding the soul into the image of God. It also has everything to do with elevating and enlarging the measure of divine grace. It has everything to do with bringing the soul into complete communion with God. It has everything to do with enriching, broadening, and maturing the soul's experience of God. A man who does not pray cannot possibly be called a Christian. There is no possible way that he can claim any right to the term or its implied significance. If he does not pray, he is a sinner, pure and simple. Prayer is the only way the soul of man can enter into fellowship and communion with the source of all Christlike spirit and energy. Therefore, if he does not pray, he is not of the household of faith.

In this study, however, we will turn our attention to one phase of prayer—persistence. It is the pressing of our desires on God with urgency and perseverance. It is praying with the kind of courage and tension that neither relaxes nor stops until its cry is heard and its cause is won.

The man who has clear views of God, has scriptural conceptions of the divine character, appreciates his privilege of approach to God, and understands his inward need of all that God has for him will be eager, outspoken, and persistent. In Scripture, the duty of prayer is advocated in terms that are barely stronger than those in which the necessity for its persistence is mentioned. Praying that influences God is said to be the outpouring of the fervent, effectual righteous man. (See James 5:16.) It is prayer on fire. It does not have a feeble, flickering flame or a momentary flash, but it shines with a vigorous, steady glow.

Prayer and Spiritual Warfare

The repeated intercessions of Abraham for the salvation of Sodom and Gomorrah present an early example of the necessity for and benefit derived from persistent prayer. The case of Jacob, wrestling all night with the angel, gives significant emphasis to the power of a dogged perseverance in prayer. It shows how, in spiritual things, persistence succeeds just as effectively as it does in matters relating to time and sense.

Moses prayed forty days and forty nights to stop the wrath of God against Israel. His example and success are a stimulus to present-day faith in its darkest hour. Elijah repeated his prayer seven times before the rain clouds appeared above the horizon and heralded the success of his prayer and the victory of his faith. On one occasion, Daniel, though faint and weak, pressed his case for three weeks before the answer and the blessing came. (See Daniel 10.)

During His earthly life, the blessed Savior spent many nights in prayer. In Gethsemane He presented the same petition three times with unshaken, urgent, yet submissive persistence. This called on every part of His soul and brought about tears and bloody sweat. His life crises were distinctly marked with, and His life victories were all won in, hours of persistent prayer. So, the servant is not greater than his Lord.

The parable of the persistent widow is a classic example of insistent prayer. We would do well to refresh our memories, at this point in our study, by reading the account from Scripture.

And he spake a parable unto them to this end, that men ought always to pray, and not to faint; saying, There was in a city a judge, which feared not God, neither regarded man: and there was a widow in that city; and she came unto him, saying, Avenge me of my

adversary. And he would not for a while: but after-
ward he said within himself, Though I fear not God,
nor regard man; yet because this widow troubleth me,
I will avenge her, lest by her continual coming she
weary me. And the Lord said, Hear what the unjust
judge saith. And shall not God avenge his own elect,
which cry day and night unto him, though he bear
long with them? I tell you he will avenge them speed-
ily.   (Luke 18:1–8)

This parable stresses the central truth of persistent prayer. The widow presses her case until the
unjust judge yields. If this parable does not teach the
necessity for persistence, it does not have any purpose or teaching. Take this one thought away, and you
have nothing left worth recording. Beyond objection,
Christ intended it to stand as evidence of the need
that exists for insistent prayer.

We have the same teaching emphasized in the
incident of the Syrophenician woman, who came to
Jesus on behalf of her daughter. Here, persistence is
shown, not as rudeness, but as the persuasive equip-
ment of humility, sincerity, and fervency. We are given
a glimpse of a woman's clinging faith, her bitter grief,
and her spiritual insight. The Master went to that
Sidonian country so that this truth could be shown
for all time: There is no cry as effective as persistent
prayer, and there is no prayer to which God surrenders
Himself so fully and so freely.

The persistence of this distressed mother won her
the victory and brought about her request. Instead
of being an offense to the Savior, it drew from Him
a word of wonder and glad surprise: *"O woman, great*
is thy faith: be it unto thee even as thou wilt" (Matt.
15:28).

Prayer and Spiritual Warfare

He who does not push his plea does not pray at all. Cold prayers have no claim on heaven and no hearing in the courts above. Fire is the life of prayer, and heaven is reached by fiery persistence rising in an ascending scale. Going back to the case of the persistent widow, we see that her widowhood, friendlessness, and weakness did not count for anything with the unjust judge. Persistence was everything. *"Because this widow troubleth me,"* he said, *"I will avenge her* [speedily], *lest...she weary me."* Because the widow imposed upon the time and attention of the unjust judge, her case was won.

God waits patiently as, day and night, His elect cry to Him. He is moved by their requests a thousand times more than this unjust judge was. A limit is set to His waiting by the persistent praying of His people, and the answer is richly given. God finds faith in His praying child. He honors this faith that stays and cries by permitting its further exercise, so that it is strengthened and enriched. Then He rewards it in abundance.

The case of the Syrophenician woman is a notable instance of successful persistence. It is one that is highly encouraging to all who pray successfully. It is a remarkable example of insistence and perseverance to ultimate victory in the face of insurmountable obstacles and hindrances. But the woman overcame them all by heroic faith and persistent spirit. Jesus had gone over into her country, *"and would have no man know it"* (Mark 7:24). But she breaks through His purpose, violates His privacy, attracts His attention, and pours out to Him a distressing appeal of need and faith. Her heart was in her prayer.

At first, Jesus appears to pay no attention to her agony and ignores her cry for relief. He gives her neither eye nor ear nor word. Silence, deep and chilling, greets her impassioned cry. But she is not turned aside or disheartened. She holds on. The disciples, offended at her unseemly noise, intercede for her, but they are silenced by the Lord's declaring that the woman is entirely outside the scope of His mission and His ministry.

But neither the failure of the disciples to gain her a hearing nor the despairing knowledge that she is barred from the benefits of His mission stop her. They serve only to lend intensity and increased boldness in her approach to Christ. She came closer, cutting her prayer in half, and fell at His feet. Worshipping Him, she made her daughter's case her own and cries with pointed brevity, *"Lord, help me!"* (Matt. 15:25). This last cry won her case. Her daughter was healed the same hour. Hopeful, urgent, and unwearied, she stays near the Master, insisting and praying until the answer is given. What a study in persistence, in earnestness. They were promoted and propelled under conditions that would have disheartened any but a heroic, constant soul.

In these parables of persistent praying, our Lord stated, for our information and encouragement, the serious difficulties that stand in the way of prayer. At the same time, He taught that persistence conquers all unfavorable circumstances and gets itself a victory over a whole host of obstacles.

He taught that an answer to prayer is conditional upon the amount of faith that goes into the petition. To test this, He will delay the answer. The superficial pray-er sinks into silence when the answer is delayed, but the man of prayer hangs on and on. The Lord recognizes and honors his faith and gives him a rich, abundant answer to his faith-evidencing, persistent prayer.

7
Prayer That Motivates God

Two thirds of the praying we do is for that which
would give us the greatest possible pleasure to
receive. It is a sort of spiritual self-indulgence in
which we engage and, as a consequence, is the
exact opposite of self-discipline. God knows all
this and keeps His children asking. In the process
of time—His time—our petitions take on another
aspect, and we, another spiritual approach. God
keeps us praying until, in His wisdom, He is ready
to answer. And no matter how long it may be
before He speaks, it is, even then, far earlier than
we have a right to expect or hope to deserve.

—Anonymous

The purpose of Christ's teachings is to declare
that men are to pray earnestly. They are to
pray with an earnestness that cannot be denied.
Heaven has listening ears only for the wholehearted
and the deeply earnest. Energy, courage, and perseverance must back the prayers that heaven respects and
that God hears.

All these qualities of soul, so essential to effectual praying, are brought out in the parable of the
man who went to his friend for bread at midnight.
(See Luke 11:5–10.) This man went on his errand

Prayer and Spiritual Warfare

with confidence. Friendship promised him success. His cry was pressing. Truly, he could not go back empty-handed. The flat refusal shamed and surprised him. Here even friendship failed! But there was still something to be tried—stern resolution and fixed determination. He would stay and pursue his demand until the door was opened and the request granted. He proceeded to do this and, by persistence, secured what ordinary requesting had failed to obtain.

The success of this man, achieved in the face of a flat denial, was used by the Savior to illustrate the need for insistence in humble prayer before the throne of heavenly grace. When the answer is not immediately given, the praying Christian must gather courage at each delay. He must urgently go forward until the answer comes. The answer is assured, if he has the faith to press his petition with vigorous faith.

Negligence, faintheartedness, impatience, and fear will be fatal to our prayers. The Father's heart, hand, infinite power, and infinite willingness to hear and give to His children are waiting for the start of our insistence.

Persistent praying is the earnest, inward movement of the heart toward God. It is throwing the entire force of the spiritual man into the exercise of prayer. Isaiah lamented that no one stirred himself to take hold of God. There was much praying done in Isaiah's time, but it was too easy, indifferent, and complacent. There were no mighty moves by souls toward God. There was no array of sanctified energies bent on reaching and grappling with God. There was no energy to draw the treasures of His grace from Him. Forceless prayers have no power to overcome difficulties, win marked results, or gain complete victories. We must win God before we can win our plea.

Prayer That Motivates God

Isaiah looked with hopeful eyes to the day when faith would flourish and there would be times of real praying. When those times would come, the watchmen would not weaken their vigilance, but would cry day and night. And those who were the Lord's remembrancers would give Him no rest. (See Isaiah 62:6–7.) Their urgent, persistent efforts would keep all spiritual interests busy and make increasing demands on God's exhaustless treasures.

Persistent praying never faints or grows weary. It is never discouraged. It never yields to cowardice but is lifted up and sustained by a hope that knows no despair and a faith that will not let go. Persistent praying has patience to wait and strength to continue. It never prepares itself to quit praying, and it refuses to get up from its knees until an answer is received.

The familiar words of the great missionary Adoniram Judson are the testimony of a man who was persistent at prayer. He said,

> I was never deeply interested in any object, never prayed sincerely and earnestly for it, but that it came at some time, no matter how distant the day. Somehow, in some shape, probably the last I would have devised, it came.

"Ask, and it shall be given you; seek, and ye shall find; knock, and it shall be opened unto you" (Matt. 7:7). These are the ringing challenges of our Lord in regard to prayer. These challenges are His explanation that true praying must stay and advance in effort and urgency until the prayer is answered and the blessing sought is received.

In the three words *ask, seek,* and *knock,* Jesus, by the order in which He places them, urges the necessity of persistence in prayer. Asking, seeking, and knocking are ascending rungs in the ladder of successful prayer. No principle is more definitely enforced by Christ than that successful prayer must have in it the quality that waits and perseveres. It must have in it the courage that never surrenders, the patience that never grows tired, and the resolution that never wavers.

In the parable of the friend at midnight, a most significant and instructive lesson in this respect is outlined. Chief among the qualities included in Christ's estimate of the highest and most successful form of praying are the following: unbeatable courage, ceaseless persistence, and stability of purpose.

Persistence is made up of intensity, perseverance, and patience. The apparent delay in answering prayer is the ground and demand of persistence. In Matthew we have the first recorded instance of the miracle of healing the blind. We have an illustration of the way in which our Lord did not seem to hear immediately those who sought Him. But the two blind men continued their crying and followed Him with their continual petition saying, *"Thou son of David, have mercy on us"* (Matt. 9:27). But He did not answer them and went into the house. The needy ones followed Him and, finally, gained their eyesight and their plea.

The case of blind Bartimaeus is a notable one in many ways. (See Mark 10:46–52.) It is especially remarkable for the show of persistence that this blind man exhibited in appealing to our Lord. His first crying, as it seems, was done as Jesus entered Jericho, and he continued it until Jesus came out of the place. It is a strong illustration of the necessity of persistent prayer. It is also an illustration of the success that comes to those who stake their all on Christ and do not give Him any peace until He grants them their hearts' desire.

Mark put the entire incident clearly before us. At first, Jesus seems not to hear. The crowd rebukes the noisy babbling of Bartimaeus. Despite the apparent unconcern of our Lord and the rebuke of an impatient, quick-tempered crowd, the blind beggar still cries. He increases the loudness of his cry until Jesus is impressed and moved. Finally, the crowd, as well as Jesus, listens to the beggar's cry and speaks in favor of his cause. He wins his case. His persistence wins even in the face of apparent neglect on the part of Jesus and despite opposition and rebuke from the surrounding crowd. His persistence won where halfhearted indifference would surely have failed.

Faith functions in connection with prayer and, of course, has its inseparable association with persistence. But the latter quality *drives* the prayer to the believing point. A persistent spirit brings a man to the place where faith takes hold, claims, and appropriates the blessing.

The absolute necessity of persistent prayer is plainly stated in the Word of God and needs to be stated and restated today. We are inclined to overlook this vital truth. Love of ease, spiritual laziness, and religious indifference all operate against this type of petitioning. Our praying, however, needs to be coaxed and pursued with an energy that never tires. It needs to have a persistency that will not be denied and a courage that never fails.

We also need to give thought to that mysterious fact of prayer—the certainty that there will be delays, denials, and seeming failures in connection with its exercise. We are to prepare for these and to permit them. However, we must not cease in our urgent praying. The praying Christian is like a brave soldier who, as the conflict grows more severe, exhibits a more superior courage than in the earlier stages of the battle. When delay and denial face him, he increases his earnest asking and does not stop until prayer prevails.

Moses furnished us with an excellent example of persistence in prayer. Instead of allowing his intimacy with God to release him from the necessity for persistence, he regarded it as something better to fit him for its exercise.

When Israel set up the golden calf, the wrath of God increased fiercely against them. Jehovah, bent on executing justice, said to Moses when He told him what He purposed to do, *"Let me alone"* (Exod. 32:10). But Moses would not let Him alone. He threw himself down before the Lord in an agony of intercession on behalf of the sinning Israelites. For forty days and nights he fasted and prayed. What a season of persistent prayer that was!

Jehovah was also angry with Aaron, who had acted as leader in this idolatrous business of the golden calf. But Moses prayed for Aaron as well as for the Israelites. If he had not prayed, both Israel and Aaron would have perished under the consuming fire of God's wrath.

That long period of pleading before God left a mighty impression on Moses. He had been in close relationship with God before, but his character never attained the greatness that marked it in the days and years following this long season of persistent intercession.

There can be no question about persistent prayer moving God and heightening human character. If we were more in agreement with God in this great command of intercession, our faces would shine more brightly. Our lives and service would possess richer qualities that earn the goodwill of humanity and bring glory to the name of God.

8
Prayer and Christian Conduct

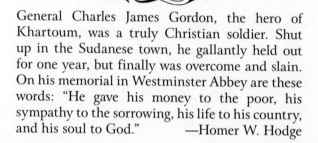

General Charles James Gordon, the hero of Khartoum, was a truly Christian soldier. Shut up in the Sudanese town, he gallantly held out for one year, but finally was overcome and slain. On his memorial in Westminster Abbey are these words: "He gave his money to the poor, his sympathy to the sorrowing, his life to his country, and his soul to God." —Homer W. Hodge

Prayer governs conduct, and conduct makes character. Conduct is what we do; character is what we are. Conduct is the outward life; character is the unseen life, hidden within, yet evidenced by that which is seen. Conduct is external, seen from without; character is internal, operating within. In the economy of grace, conduct is the offspring of character. Character is the state of the heart; conduct is its outward expression. Character is the root of the tree; conduct is the fruit it bears.

Prayer is related to all the gifts of grace. Its relationship to character and conduct is that of a helper. Prayer helps to establish character and to fashion conduct. Both, for their successful continuance, depend on prayer. There may be a certain degree of moral character and conduct independent of prayer, but there cannot be any distinctive religious character and Christian conduct without it. Prayer helps where all other aids fail. The more we pray, the better we are, and the purer and better our lives become.

The very end and purpose of the atoning work of Christ is to create religious character and make Christian conduct.

> *Who gave himself for us, that he might redeem us from all iniquity, and purify unto himself a peculiar people, zealous of good works.* (Titus 2:14)

In Christ's teaching, it is not simply works of charity and deeds of mercy that He insists upon, but inward spiritual character. This much is demanded, and nothing short of it will suffice.

In the study of Paul's epistles, there is one thing that stands out clearly and unmistakably—the insistence on holiness of heart and righteousness of life. Paul did not seek to promote what is termed "personal work." The leading theme of his letters is not deeds of charity. Rather, it is the condition of the human heart and the blamelessness of the personal life that form the burden of Paul's writings.

It is character and conduct that are most important elsewhere in the Scriptures, too. The Christian religion deals with men who are lacking spiritual character and are unholy in life. It aims to change them so that they become holy in heart and righteous in life. It aims to change bad men into good men.

Here is where prayer enters and demonstrates its wonderful ability and fruit. Prayer drives toward this specific end. In fact, without prayer, no such supernatural change in moral character can ever be effected. The change from badness to goodness is not brought about *"by works of righteousness which we have done,"* but according to God's mercy, which saves us *"by the washing of regeneration"* (Titus 3:5). This marvelous change is brought to pass through earnest, persistent, faithful prayer. Any assumed form of Christianity that does not effect this change in the hearts of men is a delusion and a snare.

The office of prayer is to change the character and conduct of men. In countless instances, change has been brought about by prayer. At this point, prayer, by its credentials, has proven its divinity. Just as it is the office of prayer to effect this, it is the major work of the church to take hold of evil men and make them good. Its mission is to change human nature and character, influence behavior, and revolutionize conduct. The church is presumed to be righteous and should be engaged in turning men to righteousness.

The church is God's factory on earth. Its primary duty is to create and foster righteous character. This is its very first business. Its primary work is not to acquire members or amass numbers. Its aim is not to get money or engage in deeds of charity and works of mercy. Its work is to produce righteousness of character and purity of the outward life.

A product reflects and partakes of the character of the manufacturer that makes it. A righteous church with a righteous purpose makes righteous men. Prayer produces cleanliness of heart and purity of life. It can produce nothing else. Unrighteous conduct is born in prayerlessness. The two go hand in hand. Prayer and sinning cannot keep company with each other. One or the other must, of necessity, stop. Get men to pray, and they will quit sinning, because prayer creates a distaste for sinning. It works so much upon the heart that evildoing becomes repugnant. It lifts the entire nature to a reverent contemplation of high and holy things.

Prayer is based on character. What we are with God determines our influence with Him. It was the inner character, not the outward appearance, of such men as Abraham, Job, David, Moses, and others that had such great influence with God in the days of old. Today, it is not so much our words, but what we really are that counts with God. Conduct affects character, of course, and counts for much in our praying.

At the same time, character affects conduct to a far greater extent and has a superior influence over prayer. Our inner life gives color to our praying.

Bad living means bad praying and, in the end, no praying at all. We pray feebly because we live feebly. The stream of prayer cannot rise higher than the fountain of living. The force of the prayer closet is made up of the energy that emerges from the flowing streams of life. The weakness of living grows out of the shallowness and shoddiness of character.

Feebleness of living reflects its weakness in the praying hours. We simply cannot talk to God strongly, intimately, and confidently unless we are living for Him, faithfully and truly. The prayer closet cannot become sanctified to God when the life is alien to His laws and purpose. We must learn this lesson well. Righteous character and Christlike conduct give us a particular and preferential standing in prayer before God. The Word gives special emphasis to the part that conduct has in imparting value to our praying.

> Then shalt thou call, and the LORD shall answer;
> thou shalt cry, and he shall say, Here I am. If thou
> take away from the midst of thee the yoke, the putting
> forth of the finger, and speaking vanity.   (Isa. 58:9)

Prayer and Christian Conduct

The wickedness of Israel and their heinous practices were definitely cited by Isaiah as the reason why God would turn His ears away from their prayers. *"And when ye spread forth your hands, I will hide mine eyes from you: yea, when ye make many prayers, I will not hear: your hands are full of blood"* (Isa. 1:15).

The same sad truth was declared by the Lord through the mouth of Jeremiah: *"Therefore pray not thou for this people, neither lift up a cry or prayer for them: for I will not hear them in the time that they cry unto me for their trouble"* (Jer. 11:14). Here, it is plainly stated that unholy conduct is a hindrance to successful praying. It is clearly suggested that, in order to have full access to God in prayer, there must be a total abandonment of conscious and premeditated sin.

We are commanded to pray, *"lifting up holy hands, without wrath and doubting"* (1 Tim. 2:8). We must pass the time we live here in a rigorous abstaining from evil if we are to keep our privilege of calling upon the Father. We cannot, by any process, divorce praying from conduct. *"And whatsoever we ask, we receive of him, because we keep his commandments, and do those things which are pleasing in his sight"* (1 John 3:22).

James declared that men ask and yet do not receive because they ask amiss and seek only the gratification of selfish desires. (See James 4:3.)

Our Lord's command to watch and pray always is to cover and guard all our conduct. Then we may come to our prayer closet with all its force secured by a vigilant guard kept over our lives.

> *And take heed to yourselves, lest at any time your hearts be overcharged with surfeiting, and drunkenness, and cares of this life, and so that day come upon you unawares.* (Luke 21:34)

Prayer and Spiritual Warfare

Quite often, Christian experience collapses on the rock of conduct. Beautiful theories are marred by ugly lives. The most difficult thing about piety, because it is the most impressive, is to be able to live it. It is the life that counts. Our praying suffers, as do other phases of our religious experience, from bad living.

In early times, preachers were ordered to preach by their lives or not preach at all. Christians everywhere ought to be reminded to pray by their lives or not pray at all. The most effective preaching is not what is heard from the pulpit, but what is proclaimed quietly, humbly, and consistently. It is preaching that exhibits its excellencies in the home and in the community. Example preaches a far more effective sermon than instruction. The best preaching, even in the pulpit, is strengthened by the preacher living a godly life.

The most effective work done by people sitting in the pews is preceded by, and accompanied with, holiness of life, separation from the world, and severance from sin. Some of the strongest appeals are made with mute lips by godly fathers and saintly mothers. These parents, around the fireside, fear God, love His cause, and daily show their children and others around them the beauties and excellencies of Christian life and conduct.

The best prepared, most eloquent sermon can be marred and rendered ineffective by questionable practices in the preacher. The most active church worker can have the labor of his hands weakened by worldliness of spirit and inconsistency of life. Men preach by their lives, not by their words. Sermons are delivered, not so much in and from a pulpit, as they are in tempers, actions, and the thousand and one incidents that crowd the pathway of daily life.

Prayer and Christian Conduct

Of course, the prayer of repentance is acceptable to God. He delights in hearing the cries of penitent sinners. But repentance involves not only sorrow for sin, but also turning away from wrongdoing and learning to do well. A repentance that does not produce a change in character and conduct is a mere sham that should deceive no one. Old things *must* pass away. All things *must* become new. (See 2 Corinthians 5:17.)

Praying that does not result in right thinking and right living is a farce. We have missed the whole office of prayer if it fails to purge character and correct conduct. We have failed entirely to understand the virtue of prayer if it does not bring about the revolutionizing of the life. In the very nature of things, we must either quit praying or quit our bad conduct. Cold, formal praying may exist side by side with bad conduct, but such praying, in God's estimation, is no praying at all. Our praying advances in power just as much as it rectifies the life. A prayerful life will grow in purity and devotion to God.

The character of the inner life is a condition of effective praying. As the life is, so the praying will be. An inconsistent life hinders praying and neutralizes what little praying we may do. Always, it is the prayer of the righteous man that avails much. (See James 5:16.) Indeed, one may go further and say that it is only the prayer of the righteous that avails anything at all, at any time. To have an eye to God's glory and to be possessed by an earnest desire to please Him in all our ways gives weight, influence, and power to prayer. To possess hands busy in His service and to have feet swift to run in the way of His commandments insure an audience with God. The oppression of our lives often breaks the force of our praying and, not infrequently, is as a door of brass in the face of prayer.

Praying must come out of a clean heart and be presented and urged with the *"lifting up* [of] *holy hands"* (1 Tim. 2:8). It must be strengthened by a life aiming, unceasingly, to obey God, to attain conformity to the divine law, and to come into submission to the divine will.

Let it not be forgotten that, while life is a condition of prayer, prayer is also the condition of righteous living. Prayer promotes righteous living and is the one great aid to uprightness of heart and life. The fruit of real praying is right living. Praying sets him who prays to the great business of working out his salvation with fear and trembling. (See Philippians 2:12.) It causes him to watch his temper, conversation, and conduct. It leads him to walk circumspectly and redeem the time. (See Ephesians 5:15–16.) It enables him to walk worthy of the vocation to which he is called, with all lowliness and meekness. (See Ephesians 4:1–2.) It gives him a high incentive to pursue his pilgrimage consistently by shunning every evil way to walk in the good. (See Psalm 199:101.)

9
Prayer and Obedience

An obedience discovered itself in John Fletcher, which I wish I could describe or imitate. It produced in him a mind ready to embrace every cross with alacrity and pleasure. He had a singular love for the lambs of the flock and applied himself with the greatest diligence to their instruction for which he had a peculiar gift.... All his fellowship with me was so mingled with prayer and praise that every employment and every meal was, as it were, perfumed therewith.

—John Wesley

Under the Mosaic law, to obey was looked upon as being *"better than sacrifice, and to hearken than the fat of rams"* (1 Sam. 15:22). In Deuteronomy 5:29, Moses represented Almighty God declaring the importance He laid upon the exercise of this quality. Referring to the waywardness of His people, He cried,

O that there were such an heart in them, that they would fear me, and keep all my commandments always, that it might be well with them, and with their children for ever!

Unquestionably, obedience is a high virtue, the quality of a soldier. To obey belongs, preeminently, to the soldier. It is his first and last lesson. He must learn how to practice it at all times without questioning or complaining. Obedience is faith in action. It is the outflow, the very test of love. *"He that hath my commandments, and keepeth them, he it is that loveth me"* (John 14:21).

Furthermore, obedience is love. *"If ye keep my commandments, ye shall abide in my love; even as I have kept my Father's commandments, and abide in his love"* (John 15:10). What a marvelous statement of the relationship created and maintained by obedience! The Son of God is held in the bosom of the Father's love by virtue of His obedience! The fact that allows the Son of God to ever abide in His Father's love is revealed in His own statement: *"For I do always those things that please him"* (John 8:29).

The gift of the Holy Spirit in full measure and in richer experience depends on loving obedience. *"If ye love me, keep my commandments"* is the Master's word. *"And I will pray the Father, and he shall give you another Comforter, that he may abide with you for ever"* (John 14:15–16).

Obedience to God is a condition of spiritual thrift, inward satisfaction, and stability of heart. Obedience opens the gates of the Holy City and gives access to the Tree of Life. *"Blessed are they that do his commandments, that they may have right to the tree of life, and may enter in through the gates into the city"* (Rev. 22:14).

What is obedience? It is doing God's will. It is keeping His commandments. How many of the commandments require obedience? To keep half of them and break the other half—is that real obedience? To keep all the commandments but one—is that obedience? The apostle James was very explicit on this point. *"Whosoever shall keep the whole law, and yet offend in one point, he is guilty of all"* (James 2:10).

The spirit that prompts a man to break one commandment is the spirit that may move him to break them all. God's commandments are a unit. To break one strikes at the principle that underlies and runs through the whole. He who does not hesitate to break a single commandment probably would, under the same stress and surrounded by the same circumstances, break them all.

Universal obedience of the race is demanded. Nothing short of absolute obedience will satisfy God. The keeping of all His commandments is the demonstration of obedience that God requires. But can we keep all of God's commandments? Can a man receive moral ability that helps him to obey every one of them? Certainly he can. By the same token, man can, through prayer, obtain ability to do this very thing.

Does God give commandments that men cannot obey? Is He so arbitrary, so severe, so unloving, that He issues commandments that cannot be obeyed? The answer is that, in all of Scripture, not a single instance is recorded of God having commanded any man to do a thing that was beyond his power. Is God so unjust and so inconsiderate to require of man something that he is unable to do? Certainly not. To infer it is to slander the character of God.

Let us think about this thought for a moment. Do earthly parents require their children to perform duties that they cannot do? Where is the father who would even think of being so unjust and so tyrannical? Is God less kind and just than faulty earthly parents? Are they better and more just than a perfect God? What a foolish and inconsistent thought!

Prayer and Spiritual Warfare

In principle, obedience to God is the same quality as obedience to earthly parents. It implies, in general, the giving up of one's own way to follow that of another. It requires the surrender of the will to the will of another. It implies the submission of oneself to the authority and requirements of a parent. Commands, either from our heavenly Father or our earthly father, are directed by love. All such commands are in the best interests of those who are commanded. God's commands are not issued in severity or tyranny. They are always issued in love and in our interests. So, it is important for us to pay attention and obey them. In other words, God has issued His commands to us in order to promote our good.

It pays, therefore, to be obedient. Obedience brings its own reward. God has ordained it so. Since He has, even human reason can realize that He would never demand what is out of our power to perform.

Obedience is love fulfilling every command. It is love expressing itself. Obedience, therefore, is not a hard demand made on us. It is not any more than the service a husband renders to his wife or a wife renders to her husband. Love delights to obey and please whom it loves. There are no hardships in love. There may be demands, but there are no irritations. There are no impossible tasks for love.

How simply and matter-of-factly John said, *"And whatsoever we ask, we receive of him, because we keep his commandments, and do those things that are pleasing in his sight"* (1 John 3:22). This is obedience, running ahead of every command. It is love, obeying by anticipation. Those who say that men are bound to commit sin because of environment, heredity, or tendency greatly err, and even sin. God's commands are not grievous (1 John 5:3). Their ways are pleasant, and their paths are peaceful. The task that falls to obedience is not a hard one. *"For my yoke is easy, and my burden is light"* (Matt. 11:30).

Far be it from our heavenly Father to demand impossibilities of His children. It is possible to please Him in all things, for He is not hard to please. He is neither a hard master nor an austere lord, *"taking up that* [he] *laid not down, and reaping that* [he] *did not sow"* (Luke 19:22). Thank God it is possible for every child of God to please his heavenly Father! It is really much easier to please Him than to please men. Moreover, we may *know* when we please Him. This is the witness of the Spirit—the inward, divine assurance given to all the children of God that they are doing their Father's will and that their ways are well pleasing in His sight.

God's commandments are righteous and founded in justice and wisdom. *"Wherefore the law is holy, and the commandment holy, and just, and good"* (Rom. 7:12). *"Just and true are thy ways, thou King of saints"* (Rev. 15:3). God's commandments, then, can be obeyed by all who seek supplies of grace that enable them to obey. These commandments must be obeyed. God's government is at stake. God's children are under obligation to obey Him. Disobedience cannot be permitted. The spirit of rebellion is the very essence of sin. It is denial of God's authority that God cannot tolerate. He has never done so. A declaration of His attitude was part of the reason why the Son of the Highest was made manifest among men.

> For what the law could not do, in that it was weak through the flesh, God sending his own Son in the likeness of sinful flesh, and for sin, condemned sin in the flesh: that the righteousness of the law might be

fulfilled in us, who walk not after the flesh, but after the Spirit. (Rom. 8:3–4)

If anyone complains that man under the Fall is too weak and helpless to obey these high commands of God, the answer is that, through the atonement of Christ, man is able to obey. The Atonement is God's enabling act. God places in us, through regeneration and the agency of the Holy Spirit, the enabling grace sufficient for all that is required of us under the Atonement. This grace is furnished without measure in answer to prayer.

So, while God commands, He, at the same time, stands pledged to give us all the necessary strength of will and grace of soul to meet His demands. Because this is true, man has no excuse for disobedience. He is immediately criticized for refusing or failing to secure necessary grace, whereby he may serve the Lord with reverence and godly fear.

Those who say it is impossible to keep God's commandments overlook one important consideration. It is the vital truth that, through prayer and faith, man's nature is changed and made partaker of the divine nature. All reluctance to obey God is taken out of him. His natural inability to keep God's commandments, growing out of his fallen and helpless state, is gloriously removed. By this radical change in his moral nature, a man receives power to obey God in every way and to yield full and glad allegiance. Then he can say, *"I delight to do thy will, O my God"* (Ps. 40:8). Not only is rebellion of the natural man removed, but he also receives a heart that gladly obeys God's Word.

There is no denying that the unrenewed man cannot obey God. But to declare that—after one is renewed by the Holy Spirit, has received a new nature, and become a child of the King—he *cannot* obey God is to assume a ridiculous attitude. It is to show a lamentable ignorance of the work and implications of the Atonement.

Absolute and perfect obedience is the state to which the man of prayer is called. *"Lifting up holy hands, without wrath and doubting"* (1 Tim. 2:8) is the condition of obedient praying. Here, inward loyalty and love, together with outward cleanliness, are set forth as accompaniments of acceptable praying.

John gave the reason for answered prayer in the passage previously quoted: *"And whatsoever we ask, we receive of him, because we keep his commandments, and do those things that are pleasing in his sight"* (1 John 3:22). Because we have said that keeping God's commandments is the reason why He answers prayer, it is reasonable to assume that we *can* keep God's commandments. We *can* do those things that are pleasing to Him. Do you think God would make the keeping of His commandments a condition of effective prayer if He knew we could not keep His statutes? *Certainly not!*

Obedience can ask with boldness at the throne of grace. Those who exercise it are the only ones who can ask after that fashion. The disobedient folk are timid in their approach and hesitant in their supplication. They are stopped by their wrongdoing. The requesting, obedient child comes into the presence of his Father with confidence and boldness. His very consciousness of obedience gives him courage and frees him from the dread born of disobedience.

To do God's will without hesitation is the joy and the privilege of the successful praying man. He who has clean hands and a pure heart can pray with confidence.

Prayer and Spiritual Warfare

In the Sermon on the Mount, Jesus said, *"Not every one that saith unto me, Lord, Lord, shall enter into the kingdom of heaven, but he that doeth the will of my Father which is in heaven"* (Matt. 7:21). To this great deliverance may be added another: *"If ye keep my commandments, ye shall abide in my love: even as I have kept my Father's commandments, and abide in his love"* (John 15:10).

"The Christian's trade," said Martin Luther, "is prayer." But the Christian has another trade to learn before he proceeds to learn the secrets of the trade of prayer. He must learn well the trade of perfect obedience to the Father's will. Obedience follows love, and prayer follows obedience. The business of *real* obedience to God's commandments inseparably accompanies the business of *real* praying.

One who has been disobedient may pray. He may pray for pardoning mercy and the peace of his soul. He may come to God's feet with tears, confession, and a penitent heart. God will hear him and answer his prayer. This kind of praying does not belong to the child of God, but to the penitent sinner, who has no other way to approach God. It is the possession of the unjustified soul, not of him who has been saved and reconciled to God.

An obedient life helps prayer. It speeds prayer to the throne. God cannot help hearing the prayer of an obedient child. He has always heard His obedient children when they have prayed. Unquestioning obedience counts much in the sight of God, at the throne of heavenly grace. It acts like the flowing tides of many rivers. It gives volume and fullness of flow, as well as power, to the prayer closet. An obedient life is not simply a reformed life. It is not the old life primed and repainted. It is not a superficial church-going life or a flurry of activities. Neither is it an external conformation to the dictates of public morality. Far more than all this is combined in a truly obedient Christian God-fearing life.

A life of full obedience, a life that is settled on the most intimate terms with God, offers no hindrance to the prayer closet. Where the will is in full conformity to God's will and the outward life shows the fruit of righteousness like Aaron and Hur, such a life lifts up and sustains the hands of prayer.

If you have an earnest desire to pray well, you must learn how to obey well. If you have a desire to learn to pray, then you must have an earnest desire to learn how to do God's will. If you desire to pray to God, you must first have a consuming desire to obey Him. If you want to have free access to God in prayer, then every obstacle in the nature of sin or disobedience must be removed.

God delights in the prayers of obedient children. Requests coming from the lips of those who delight to do His will reach His ears with great speed. They incline Him to answer them promptly and abundantly. In themselves, tears are not rewarding. Yet, they have their uses in prayer. Tears should baptize our place of supplication.

The person who has never wept concerning his sins has never really prayed over his sins. Sometimes tears are a prodigal's only plea. But tears are for the past, for the sin and wrongdoing. There is another step and stage waiting to be taken. That step is unquestioning obedience. Until it is taken, prayer for blessing and continued sustenance will be of no avail.

Everywhere in Scripture, God is represented as disapproving disobedience and condemning sin. This is as true in the lives of His elect as it is in the lives of sinners. Nowhere does He approve of sin or excuse disobedience. God puts the emphasis always upon obedience to His commands. Obedience to them brings blessing. Disobedience meets with disaster. This is true in the Word of God from the beginning to the end. It is because of this that the men of prayer in the Bible had such influence with God. Obedient men have always been the closest to God. They are the ones who have prayed well and have received great things from God. They have brought great things to pass.

Obedience to God counts tremendously in the realm of prayer. This fact cannot be emphasized too much or too often. To plead for a faith that tolerates sinning is to cut the ground out from under the feet of effective praying. To excuse sinning by the plea that obedience to God is not possible to unregenerate men is to discount the character of the new birth and to place men where effective praying is not possible. At one time Jesus spoke out with a very pertinent and personal question that strikes right to the core of disobedience. He asked, *"Why call ye me, Lord, Lord, and do not the things which I say?"* (Luke 6:46).

He who prays must obey. The person who wants to get anything out of his prayers must be in perfect harmony with God. Prayer puts a spirit of obedience in those who sincerely pray. The spirit of disobedience is not of God and does not belong to God's praying people.

An obedient life is a great help to prayer. In fact, an obedient life is a necessity to prayer. The absence of an obedient life makes prayer an empty performance. A penitent sinner seeks pardon and salvation and has an answer to his prayers, even with a life stained with sin. However, God's royal intercessors

Prayer and Obedience

come before Him with royal lives. Holy living promotes holy praying. God's intercessors, *"lifting up holy
hands"* (1 Tim. 2:8), are the symbols of righteous, obedient lives.

10
Prayer and Full Surrender

———— •◦⟨∞⟩◦• ————

Many exemplary men have I known, holy in
heart and life, within my four score years. But
one equal to John Fletcher—one so inwardly and
outwardly obedient and devoted to God—I have
not known.   —John Wesley

I t is important to note that the praying that is given
such a transcendent position, and from which great
results are attributed, is not simply the saying of
prayers, but holy praying. This is the *"prayers of the
saints"* (Rev. 8:4). This is the prayers of the holy men
and women of God. Behind such praying, giving to
it energy and flame, are men and women who are
wholly devoted to God. They are entirely separated
from sin and fully separated to God. They always give
energy, force, and strength to praying.

Our Lord Jesus Christ excelled in praying because
He was supreme in saintliness. Entire dedication to
God and full surrender, which carry the whole being
in a flame of holy consecration, give wings to faith
and energy to prayer. Full surrender opens the door to
the throne of grace. It brings strong influence to bear
on Almighty God.

The *"lifting up* [of] *holy hands"* (1 Tim. 2:8) is
essential to Christlike praying. It is not, however, a

holiness that only dedicates a closet to God. It does not merely set apart an hour to Him. It is a consecration that takes hold of the entire man. It dedicates the whole life to God.

Our Lord Jesus Christ, who was *"holy, harmless, undefiled, separate from sinners"* (Heb. 7:26), had ready access to God in prayer. He had this free, full access because of His unquestioning obedience to His Father. Throughout His earthly life, His supreme care and desire was to do the will of His Father. This fact, coupled with another—the consciousness of having so ordered His life—gave Him confidence and assurance. It enabled Him to draw near to the throne of grace with unlimited confidence born of obedience, promised acceptance, audience, and answer.

Loving obedience puts us where we can ask anything in His name. It gives us the assurance that He will do it. (See John 14:14.) Loving obedience brings us into the prayer realm. It makes us beneficiaries of the wealth of Christ. We receive the riches of His grace through the Holy Spirit, who will abide with us and be in us. Cheerful obedience to God qualifies us to pray effectively.

This obedience that qualifies and is the forerunner of prayer must be loving and constant. It is always doing the Father's will and cheerfully following the path of God's commands.

In King Hezekiah's situation, it was a potent plea that changed God's decree that he should die and not live. The stricken ruler called upon God to remember how he had walked before Him in truth and with a perfect heart. With God, this counted. He listened carefully to the petition. As a result, death found its approach to Hezekiah barred for fifteen years.

Prayer and Full Surrender

Jesus learned obedience in the school of suffering. At the same time, He learned prayer in the school of obedience. Just as it is the prayer of a righteous man that avails much, so it is righteousness that is obedience to God. A righteous man is an obedient man. He can pray effectively. He can accomplish great things when he goes to his knees.

Remember that true praying is not mere sentiment, poetry, or eloquent speech. It does not consist of saying in sweet tones, "Lord, Lord." Prayer is not a mere form of words. It is not just calling upon a name. *Prayer is obedience.* It is founded on the unbending rock of obedience to God. Only those who obey have the right to pray. Behind the praying must be the doing. It is the constant doing of God's will in daily life that gives prayer its potency.

Our Lord plainly taught,

> *Not every one that saith unto me, Lord, Lord, shall enter the kingdom of heaven; but he that doeth the will of my Father which is in heaven. Many will say to me in that day, Lord, Lord, have we not prophesied in thy name? and in thy name have cast out devils? and in thy name done many wonderful works? And then will I profess unto them, I never knew you: depart from me, ye that worketh iniquity.* (Matt. 7:21–23)

No name, however precious and powerful, can protect and give effectiveness to prayer that is unaccompanied by doing God's will. Neither can the doing, without the praying, protect from divine disapproval. If the will of God does not master the life, the praying will be nothing but sickly sentiment. If prayer does not inspire, sanctify, and direct our work, then self-will enters and ruins both the work and worker.

Prayer and Spiritual Warfare

How many great misconceptions there are of the true elements and functions of prayer! There are many who earnestly desire to obtain answers to their prayers but who go unrewarded and unblessed. They fix their minds on some promise of God. Then they endeavor by stubborn perseverance to summon enough faith to lay hold of it and claim it. This fixing the mind on some great promise may help in strengthening faith, but persistent and urgent prayer—prayer that expects and waits until faith grows exceedingly—must be added to this promise. Who is able and competent to do such praying except the man who readily, cheerfully, and continually obeys God?

Faith, in its highest form, is the attitude as well as the act of a soul surrendered to God. His Word and His Spirit dwell in that soul. It is true that faith must exist in some form or another in order to prompt praying. However, in its strongest form and in its greatest results, faith is the fruit of prayer. It is true that faith increases the ability and efficiency of prayer. It is likewise true that prayer increases the ability and effectiveness of faith. Prayer and faith work, act, and react one upon the other.

Obedience to God helps faith as no other attribute possibly can. When there is absolute recognition of the validity and supremacy of the divine commands, faith ceases to be an almost superhuman task. It requires no straining to exercise it. Obedience to God makes it easy to believe and trust God. Where the spirit of obedience totally saturates the soul and the will is perfectly surrendered to God, faith becomes a reality. It also does this where there is a fixed, unalterable purpose to obey God. Faith then becomes almost involuntary. After obedience it is the next natural step. It is easily and readily taken. The difficulty

Prayer and Full Surrender

in prayer then is not with faith but with obedience, which is faith's foundation.

If we want to pray well and get the most out of our praying, we must look at our obedience. We must look at the secret springs of action and the loyalty of our hearts to God. Obedience is the groundwork of effective praying. This brings us near to God.

The lack of obedience in our lives breaks down our praying. Quite often our lives are in rebellion. This places us where praying is almost impossible, except for pardoning mercy. Disobedient living produces extremely poor praying. Disobedience shuts the door of the prayer closet. It bars the way to the Holy of Holies. No man can pray—really pray—who does not obey.

Our will must be surrendered to God as a primary condition to all successful praying. Everything about us receives its coloring from our innermost character. Our secret will determines our character and controls our conduct. Our will, therefore, plays an important part in all successful praying. There can be no rich, true praying when the will is not wholly and fully surrendered to God. This unswerving loyalty to God is an utterly indispensable condition of the best, truest, and most effective praying. We have simply to

> Trust and obey.
> For *there's no other way*
> To be happy in Jesus,
> But to trust and *obey!*

11
Prayer and Spiritual Warfare

———— •·•◄⟨∽⟩►•·• ————

David Brainerd was pursued by unearthly
adversaries who were resolved to rob him of his
reward. He knew he must never take off his
armor, but lie down to rest with his [sandals]
laced. The stains that marred the perfection of
his lustrous dress and the spots of rust on his
gleaming shield are imperceptible to us, but they
were to him the source of much sorrow and
ardency of yearning. —*The Life of David Brainerd*

The description of the Christian soldier given by
Paul in Ephesians 6 is compact and comprehensive. He is seen as always being in the conflict,
which has many fluctuating seasons. There are seasons of prosperity and adversity, lightness and dark-
ness, victory and defeat. He is to pray in all seasons
and with all prayer. This is to be added to the armor
when he goes into battle. At all times, he is to have
the full armor of prayer. The Christian soldier, if he
fights to win, must pray much. Only by this means is
he able to defeat his long-standing enemy, Satan, and
his many agents. *"Praying always with all prayer"* (Eph.
6:18) is the divine direction given to him. This covers
all seasons and includes all manner of praying.

Prayer and Spiritual Warfare

Christian soldiers, fighting the good fight of faith (1 Tim. 6:12), have access to a place of retreat where they continually go for prayer. *"Praying always with all prayer"* is a clear statement of the essential need of much praying. It is also a statement of many kinds of praying, by him who, fighting the good fight of faith, wins out over all his foes in the end.

The Revised Version puts it this way:

> *With all prayer and supplication praying at all seasons in the Spirit...for all the saints, and on my behalf, that utterance may be given unto me in opening my mouth, to make known with boldness the mystery of the gospel, for which I am an ambassador in chains; that in it I may speak boldly, as I ought to speak.* (Eph. 6:18–20)

It cannot be said too often that the life of a Christian is warfare, an intense conflict, a lifelong contest. It is a battle fought against invisible foes who are ever alert and seeking to entrap, deceive, and ruin the souls of men. The Bible calls men to life, not a picnic or holiday. It is no pastime or pleasure excursion. It entails effort, wrestling, and struggling. It demands putting out the full energy of the spirit in order to frustrate the foe and to come out, at last, more than a conqueror. It is no primrose path, no rose-scented flirting. From start to finish, it is war. The Christian warrior is compelled from the hour he first draws his sword to *"endure hardness, as a good soldier"* (2 Tim. 2:3).

What a misconception many people have of the Christian life! How little the average church member appears to know of the character of the conflict and of its demands on him! How ignorant he seems to be of the enemies he must encounter if he is to serve God faithfully, succeed in getting to heaven, and receive the crown of life! He scarcely seems to realize that the world, the flesh, and the devil will oppose his onward march. He hardly realizes that they will defeat him utterly, unless he gives himself to constant vigilance and unceasing prayer.

The Christian soldier does not wrestle against flesh and blood, but against spiritual wickedness in high places (Eph. 6:12). Or, as the scriptural margin note in reads, "wicked spirits in high places" (RV, mg). What a fearful array of forces are set against him! They desire to impede his way through the wilderness of this world to the doors of the Celestial City! It is no surprise, therefore, to find Paul, who understood the character of the Christian life so well, carefully and plainly urging Christians to *"put on the whole armour of God"* (v. 11). It is not surprising that Paul, who was so thoroughly informed as to the malignity and number of the foes that the disciple of the Lord must encounter, urged us to pray *"with all prayer and supplication in the Spirit"* (v. 18). The present generation would be wise if all who profess our faith could be persuaded to realize this all-important, vital truth, which is absolutely indispensable to a successful Christian life.

It is just at this point in today's Christianity that one may find its greatest defect. There is little or nothing of the soldier element in it. The discipline, self-denial, spirit of hardship, and determination so prominent in and belonging to the military life are lacking. Yet, the Christian life is warfare, all the way.

How comprehensive, pointed, and striking are all Paul's directions to the Christian soldier who is bent on defeating the devil and saving his soul alive. First of all, he must possess a clear idea of the character of the life into which he has entered. Then, he must know something of his foes—the adversaries of his immortal soul—their strength, their skill, their viciousness.

Knowing something of the character of the enemy and realizing the need of preparation to overcome them, he is prepared to hear the apostle's decisive conclusion:

> *Finally, my brethren, be strong in the Lord, and in the power of his might. Put on the whole armour of God, that ye may be able to stand against the wiles of the devil....Wherefore take unto you the whole armour of God, that ye may be able to withstand in the evil day, and having done all, to stand.*   (Eph. 6:10–11, 13)

All these directions end in a climax, and that climax is prayer. How can the brave warrior for Christ be made braver still? How can the strong soldier be made stronger still? How can the victorious fighter be made still more victorious?

Here are Paul's explicit directions to that end: *"Praying always with all prayer and supplication in the Spirit, and watching thereunto with all perseverance and supplication for all saints"* (Eph. 6:18).

Prayer, and more prayer, adds to the fighting qualities and the more certain victories of God's good, fighting men. The power of prayer is most forceful on the battlefield in the midst of the noise and strife of the conflict. Paul was preeminently a soldier of the cross. For him, life was no flowery bed of ease. He was no parading, holiday soldier, whose only business was to put on a uniform for special occasions. His was a life of intense conflict, the facing of many adversaries, the exercise of unsleeping vigilance and constant effort. And in sight of the end, we hear him as he chanted his final song of victory, *"I have fought a good fight"* (2 Tim. 4:7). Reading between the lines, we see that he was more than a conqueror!

Paul indicated the nature of his soldier life, giving us some views of the kind of praying needed for such a career. He wrote,

> *Now I beseech you, brethren, for the Lord Jesus Christ's sake, and for the love of the Spirit, that ye strive together with me in your prayers to God for me; that I may be delivered from them that do not believe in Judaea.* (Rom. 15:30–31)

Paul *had* foes in Judea—foes who surrounded and opposed him in the form of unbelieving men, and this, added to other weighty reasons, led him to urge the Roman Christians to strive with him in prayer. That word *strive* indicates wrestling, the putting forth of great effort. This is the kind of effort and spirit that must possess the Christian soldier.

Here is a great soldier, in the great struggle, faced by malignant forces who seek his ruin. His strength is almost gone. What reinforcements can he count on? What can give help and bring success to a warrior in such a pressing emergency? It is a critical moment in the conflict. What strength can be added to the energy of his own prayers? The answer is—the prayers of others, even the prayers of his fellow believers who were at Rome. These, he believes, will bring him additional aid. He can then win his fight, overcome his adversaries, and, ultimately, prevail.

The Christian soldier is to pray in all seasons and under all circumstances. His praying must be arranged in order to cover his times of peace as well as his hours of active conflict. It must be available in his marching and his fighting. Prayer must diffuse all effort, permeate all ventures, decide all issues. The Christian soldier must be as intense in his praying as in his fighting, for his victories will depend much more on his praying than on his fighting.

Fervent supplication must be added to steady resolve. Prayer and supplication must supplement the armor of God. The Holy Spirit must aid the supplication with His own strenuous plea. And the soldier must pray in the Spirit. In this, as in other forms of warfare, eternal vigilance is the price of victory. Thus, watchfulness and perseverance must mark every activity of the Christian warrior.

The soldier's prayer must reflect his profound concern for the success and well-being of the whole army. The battle is not altogether a personal matter. Victory cannot be achieved for self alone. There is a sense in which the entire army of Christ is involved. The cause of God, His saints, their woes and trials, their duties and crosses—all should find a pleading voice in the Christian soldier when he prays. He does not dare to limit his praying to himself. Nothing dries up spiritual blessings so certainly and completely, nothing poisons the fountain of spiritual life so effectively, and nothing acts in such deadly fashion as selfish praying.

Note carefully that the Christian's armor will avail him nothing unless prayer is added. This is the pivot, the connecting link of the armor of God. This holds it together and renders it effective. God's true soldier plans his campaigns, arranges his battle forces, and conducts his conflicts with prayer. Prayer is all-important and absolutely essential to victory. Prayer should so saturate the life that every breath becomes a petition, every sigh a supplication. The Christian soldier must always be fighting. He should, of sheer necessity, be always praying.

Prayer and Spiritual Warfare

The Christian soldier is compelled to constant guard duty. He is faced by a foe who never sleeps, who is always alert, and who is ever prepared to take advantage of the fortunes of war. Watchfulness is a fundamental principle with Christ's warrior; *"watch and pray"* (Matt. 26:41) is forever sounding in his ears. He cannot dare to be asleep at his post. Such a lapse brings him not only under the displeasure of the Captain of his salvation, but also exposes him to added danger. Watchfulness, therefore, imperatively constitutes the duty of the soldier of the Lord.

In the New Testament, there are three different words that are translated "watch." The first means "absence of sleep" and implies a wakeful frame of mind as opposed to listlessness. It is a command to keep awake, attentive, and vigilant. The second word means "fully awake"—a state induced by some rousing, active, cautious effort lest, through carelessness or laziness, some destructive calamity should suddenly evolve. The third word means "to be calm and collected in spirit," unemotional, untouched by confusing circumstances, cautious against all pitfalls and diversions.

All three words were used by Paul. Two of them are used in connection with prayer. Watchfulness intensified is a necessity for prayer. Watchfulness must guard and cover the whole spiritual man and prepare him for prayer. Everything resembling unpreparedness or non-vigilance is death to prayer.

In Ephesians 6:18, Paul gave prominence to the duty of constant watchfulness, *"watching thereunto with all perseverance and supplication."* "Watch," he said, *"watch,* WATCH!"

Sleepless alertness is the price one must pay for victory over his spiritual foes. Rest assured that the devil never falls asleep. He ever *"walketh about, seeking whom he may devour"* (1 Pet. 5:8). Just as a shepherd must never be careless or unwatchful lest the wolf devour his sheep, so the Christian soldier must have his eyes wide open, implying his possession of a spirit that neither slumbers nor grows careless. The inseparable companions and safeguards of prayer are vigilance and watchfulness. In writing to the Colossians, Paul bracketed these inseparable qualities together: *"Continue in prayer, and watch in the same with thanksgiving"* (Col. 4:2).

When will Christians more thoroughly learn the twofold lesson that they are called to a great warfare and that, in order to get the victory, they must give themselves to unsleeping watchfulness and unceasing prayer? *"Be sober, be vigilant; because your adversary the devil, as a roaring lion, walketh about, seeking whom he may devour"* (1 Pet. 5:8).

God's church is a militant host. Its warfare is with unseen forces of evil. God's people compose an army fighting to establish His kingdom in the earth. Their aim is to destroy the sovereignty of Satan and, over its ruins, erect the kingdom of God, which is *"righteousness, and peace, and joy in the Holy Ghost"* (Rom. 14:17). This militant army is composed of individual soldiers of the cross. The armor of God is needed for defense, and added prayer crowns the entire army.

Prayer is too simple, too obvious a duty, to need definition. Necessity gives being and shape to prayer. Its importance is so absolute that the Christian soldier's life, in all the breadth and intensity of it, should be one of prayer. The entire life of a Christian soldier—its being, intention, implication, and action—are all dependent on its being a life of prayer. Without prayer—no matter what else he has—the Christian soldier's life will be feeble and ineffective. Without prayer, he is an easy prey for his spiritual enemies.

Unless prayer has an important place in a Christian's life, his experience and influence will be powerless. Without prayer the Christian graces will wither and die. Without prayer, we may add, preaching is futile and fruitless. Christ is the Lawgiver of prayer, and Paul is His apostle of prayer. Both declare its primary importance and demonstrate the fact of its necessity. Their prayer directions cover all places, include all times, and comprehend all things. How, then, can the Christian soldier hope or dream of victory, unless he is fortified by its power? How can he fail if in addition to putting on the armor of God he is, at all times and seasons, *watching thereunto with all perseverance and supplication for all saints"* (Eph. 6:18)?

12
Prayer and God's Promises

In the Scriptures, we constantly encounter such words as "field," "seed," "sower," "reaper," "seedtime," "harvest." Employing such metaphors interprets a fact of nature by a parable of grace. The field is the world and the good seed is the Word of God. Whether the Word be spoken or written, it is the power of God unto salvation. In our work of evangelism, the whole world is our field, every creature the object of effort, and every book and tract, a seed of God. —David Fant, Jr.

God's Word is a record of prayer—of praying men and their achievements, of the divine warrant of prayer, and of the encouragement given to those who pray. No one can read the instances, commands, and examples of statements that concern themselves with prayer without realizing that the cause of God and the success of His work in this world are committed to prayer. Praying men have been God's appointed officers on earth. Prayerless men have never been used by Him.

A reverence for God's holy name is closely related to a high regard for His Word. This hallowing of God's name, the ability to do His will on earth as it is done in heaven, and the establishment and glory of God's kingdom are as much involved in prayer as when Jesus taught men the universal prayer. That *"men ought always to pray, and not to faint"* (Luke 18:1) is as fundamental to God's cause today as when Jesus Christ enshrined that great truth in the immortal setting of the parable of the persistent widow.

As God's house is called *"the house of prayer"* (Matt. 21:13), because prayer is the most important of its holy offices, so, by the same token, the Bible may be called the book of prayer. Prayer is the great theme and content of its message to mankind.

God's Word is the basis of, the directory of, and the prayer of faith. Paul said,

> *Let the word of Christ dwell in you richly in all wisdom; teaching and admonishing one another in psalms and hymns and spiritual songs, singing with grace in your hearts to the Lord.* (Col. 3:16)

As the Word of Christ dwells richly in us, we become transformed. The result is that we become praying Christians. Faith is constructed of the Word and the Spirit, and faith is the body and substance of prayer.

In many of its aspects, prayer is dependent on the Word of God. Jesus says, *"If ye abide in me, and my words abide in you, ye shall ask what ye will, and it shall be done unto you"* (John 15:7).

The Word of God is the support upon which the lever of prayer is placed and by which things are mightily moved. God has committed Himself, His purpose, and His promise to prayer. His Word becomes the basis and the inspiration of our praying. Under certain circumstances, persistent prayer may bring additional assurance of His promises. It is said of the old saints that they *"through faith...obtained promises"* (Heb. 11:33).

Prayer and God's Promises

There would seem to be the capacity in prayer for going beyond the Word, beyond His promise, and into the very presence of God Himself.

Jacob wrestled, not so much with a promise, as with the Promiser. We must take hold of the Promiser, or else the promise is useless. Prayer may well be defined as the force that vitalizes and energizes the Word of God, by taking hold of God Himself. By taking hold of the Promiser, prayer releases the personal promise. *"There is none...that stirreth up himself to take hold of* [me]" (Isa. 64:7) is God's sad lament. *"Let him take hold of my strength, that he may make peace with me"* (Isa. 27:5) is God's recipe for prayer.

By scriptural authority, prayer may be divided into the petition of faith and that of submission. The prayer of faith is based on the written Word, for *"faith cometh by hearing, and hearing by the word of God"* (Rom. 10:17). It inevitably receives its answer—the very thing for which it prays.

The prayer of submission is without a definite word of promise, so to speak. However, it takes hold of God with a lowly and contrite spirit and asks and pleads with Him for that which the soul desires. Abraham had no definite promise that God would spare Sodom. Moses had no definite promise that God would spare Israel. On the contrary, there was the declaration of His wrath and of His purpose to destroy. Still, the devoted leader gained his plea with God when he interceded for the Israelites with incessant prayers and many tears. Daniel had no definite promise that God would reveal to him the meaning of the king's dream, but he prayed specifically, and God answered definitely.

The Word of God is made effective and operative by the process and practice of prayer. The Word of the Lord came to Elijah, *"Go, show thyself unto Ahab; and I will send rain upon the earth"* (1 Kings 18:1). Elijah showed himself to Ahab, but the answer to his prayer did not come until he had pressed his fiery prayer upon the Lord seven times.

Paul had the definite promise from Christ that He would deliver him *"from the people, and from the Gentiles"* (Acts 26:17). Yet, we find that he exhorted the Romans in an urgent and solemn manner concerning this very matter:

> *Now I beseech you, brethren, for the Lord Jesus Christ's sake, and for the love of the Spirit, that ye strive together with me in your prayers to God for me; that I may be delivered from them that do not believe in Judaea; and that my service which I have for Jerusalem may be accepted of the saints.*
>
> (Rom. 15:30–31)

The Word of God is a great help in prayer. If it is lodged and written in our hearts, it will form an outflowing current of prayer, full and irresistible. Promises, stored in the heart, are to be the fuel from which prayer receives life and warmth. Just as coal, which has been stored in the earth, gives us comfort on stormy days and wintry nights, the Word of God stored in our hearts is the food by which prayer is nourished and made strong. Prayer, like man, cannot live by bread alone, *"but by every word that proceedeth out of the mouth of God"* (Matt. 4:4).

Unless the vital forces of prayer are supplied by God's Word, prayer, though earnest, even vociferous in its urgency, is flabby and void in reality. The absence of vital force in praying can be traced to the absence of a constant supply of God's Word to repair the waste and renew the life. He who wants to learn to pray well must first study God's Word and store it in his memory and thought.

When we consult God's Word, we find that no duty is more binding, more exacting, than that of prayer. On the other hand, we discover that no privilege is more exalted, no habit more richly owned of God. No promises are more radiant, more abounding, more explicit, more often reiterated, than those that are attached to prayer. *"All things whatsoever"* are received by prayer because *"all things whatsoever"* (Matt. 21:22) are promised. There is no limit to the provisions included in the promises to prayer and no exclusion from its promises. *"For every one that asketh receiveth"* (Luke 11:10). The word of our Lord is to this all-embracing effect: *"If ye shall ask any thing in my name, I will do it"* (John 14:14).

Here are some of the comprehensive and exhaustive statements of the Word of God about prayer, the things to be taken in by prayer, and the strong promise made in answer to prayer: *"Pray without ceasing"* (1 Thess. 5:17); *"continue in prayer"* (Col. 4:2); *"continuing instant in prayer"* (Rom. 12:12); *"in every thing by prayer...let your requests be made known unto God"* (Phil. 4:6); *"always to pray, and not to faint"* (Luke 18:1); *"men* [should] *pray every where"* (1 Tim. 2:8); *"praying always with all prayer and supplication"* (Eph. 6:18).

What clear and strong statements those are that are put in the divine record to furnish us with a sure basis of faith and to urge, constrain, and encourage us to pray! How wide the range of prayer in the divine revelation! How these Scriptures incite us to seek the God of prayer, with all our needs, with all our burdens!

In addition to these statements left on record for our encouragement, the sacred pages teem with facts, examples, incidents, and observations, stressing the importance and the absolute necessity of prayer and putting emphasis on its all-prevailing power.

The greatest benefit of the rich promises of the Word of God should humbly be received by us and put to the test. The world will never receive the full benefits of the Gospel until this is done. Neither Christian experience nor Christian living will be what they ought to be until these divine promises have been fully tested by those who pray. By prayer, we bring these promises of God's holy will into the realm of the actual and the real.

If asked what is to be done in order to render God's promises real, the answer is that we must pray, until the words of the promise are fulfilled.

God's promises are too large to be mastered by aimless praying. When we examine ourselves, we discover that our praying does not rise to the demands of the situation. It is so limited that it is little more than a mere oasis amid the waste and desert of the world's sin. Who of us, in our praying, measures up to the promises of our Lord? *"Verily, verily, I say unto you, He that believeth on me, the works that I do shall he do also; and greater works than these shall he do; because I go unto my Father"* (John 14:12).

How comprehensive, how far reaching, how all-embracing! How much is here, for the glory of God, how much for the good of man! How much for the manifestation of Christ's enthroned power, how much for the reward of abundant faith! How great and gracious are the results that grow from the exercise of believing prayer!

Look at another of God's great promises and discover how we may be strengthened by the Word as we pray and on what firm ground we may stand to make our petitions to our God: *"If ye abide in me, and my words abide in you, ye shall ask what ye will, and it shall be done unto you"* (John 15:7). In these comprehensive words, God turns Himself over to the will of His people. When Christ becomes our all in all, prayer lays God's treasures at our feet.

Early Christianity had an easy and practical solution to the situation. The first Christians received all that God had to give. That simple, short solution is recorded in 1 John 3:22: *"Whatsoever we ask, we receive of him, because we keep his commandments, and do those things that are pleasing in his sight."*

Prayer coupled with loving obedience is the answer to all ends and all things. Prayer joined to the Word of God hallows and makes sacred all God's gifts. Prayer is not simply to receive things from God, but to make holy those things that already have been received of Him. It is not merely to *receive* a blessing, but also to be able to *give* a blessing. Prayer makes common things holy and secular things sacred. It receives things from God with thanksgiving and hallows them with thankful hearts and devoted service.

In 1 Timothy 4:4–5, Paul gave us these words: *"For every creature of God is good, and nothing to be refused, if it be received with thanksgiving: for it is sanctified by the word of God and prayer."* God's good gifts are to be holy, not only by God's creative power, but also because they are made holy to us by prayer. We receive them, appropriate them, and sanctify them by prayer.

Doing God's will—having His Word abiding in us—is an imperative of effective praying. But, it may be asked, how are we to know what God's will is? The answer is by studying His Word (see 2 Timothy 2:15), by hiding it in our hearts (see Psalm 119:11), and by letting the Word dwell in us richly. (See

Colossians 3:16.) *"The entrance of thy words giveth light"* (Ps. 119:130).

To know God's will in prayer, we must be filled with God's Spirit, who makes intercession for the saints according to the will of God. (See Romans 8:27.) To be filled with God's Spirit, to be filled with God's Word, is to know God's will. It is to be put in such a frame of mind and state of heart that it will enable us to read and correctly interpret the purposes of the infinite. Such filling of the heart with the Word and the Spirit gives us an insight into the will of the Father. It enables us to rightly discern His will and puts a disposition of mind and heart within us to make it the guide and compass of our lives.

Epaphras prayed that the Colossians might stand *"perfect and complete in all the will of God"* (Col. 4:12). This is proof positive that not only can we know the will of God, but that we can know *all* the will of God. And not only can we know all the will of God, but we can *do* all the will of God. In addition, we can do all the will of God as an established habit instead of an occasional impulse. Still further, it shows us that we not only can do the will of God externally, but from the heart, cheerfully, without holding back from the intimate presence of the Lord.

13
Prayer and the Word of God

Some years ago a man was traveling in the wilds of Kentucky. He had with him a large sum of money and was well armed. He stayed at a log house one night but was much concerned with the rough appearance of the men who came and went from this abode. He retired early, but not to sleep. At midnight he heard the dogs barking furiously and the sound of someone entering the cabin. Peering through a chink in the boards of his room, he saw a stranger with a gun in his hand. Another man sat before the fire. The traveler concluded they were planning to rob him and prepared to defend himself and his property. Presently the newcomer took down a copy of the Bible, read a chapter aloud, and then knelt down and prayed. The traveler dismissed his fears, put his revolver away, and lay down to sleep peacefully until morning light. And all because a Bible was in the cabin and its owner a man of prayer.

—Rev. F. F. Shoup

Prayer means the success of the preaching of the Word. Paul clearly taught this in that familiar and pressing request he made to the Thessalonians: *"Finally, brethren, pray for us, that the word of the Lord may have free course, and be glorified"* (2 Thess. 3:1).

Prayer opens the way for the Word of God to run without hindrance. It creates the atmosphere that is favorable for the Word to accomplish its purpose. Prayer puts wheels under God's Word and gives wings to the angel of the Lord *"having the everlasting gospel to preach unto them that dwell on the earth, and to every nation, and kindred, and tongue, and people"* (Rev. 14:6). Prayer greatly helps the Word of the Lord.

The parable of the sower is a notable study of preaching, showing its differing effects and describing the diversity of hearers. The wayside hearers are many. The soil lies unprepared either by previous thought or prayer. As a consequence, the enemy easily takes away the seed (which is the Word of God). Dissipating all good impressions, Satan renders the work of the sower futile. If only the hearers would prepare the ground of their hearts beforehand by prayer and meditation, much of the current sowing would be fruitful.

The same applies to the stony-ground and thorny-ground hearers. Although the Word lodges in their hearts and begins to sprout, yet all is lost, chiefly because there is no prayer or watchfulness or cultivation following. The good-ground hearers are profited by the sowing, simply because their minds have been prepared for the reception of the seed. After hearing, they have cultivated the seed sown in their hearts by the exercise of prayer. All this gives particular emphasis to the conclusion of this striking parable: *"Take heed therefore how ye hear"* (Luke 8:18). In order that we can heed how we hear, we must give ourselves continually to prayer.

We have to believe that the success and effect of God's Word depend on prayer. *"So shall my word be that*

Prayer and the Word of God

goeth forth out of my mouth: it shall not return unto me void, but it shall...prosper in the thing whereto I sent it" (Isa. 55:11).

In Psalm 19, David magnified the Word of God in six statements concerning it. The Word converts the soul, makes the simple wise, rejoices the heart, enlightens the eyes, endures eternally, and is altogether true and righteous. The Word of God is perfect, sure, right, and pure. It is heart-searching and, at the same time, purifying in its effect.

It is no surprise that after considering the deep spirituality of the Word of God, its power to search the inner nature of man, and its deep purity, the psalmist should close his dissertation with this passage:

> *Who can understand his errors? cleanse thou me from secret faults. Keep back thy servant also from presumptuous sins; let them not have dominion over me....Let the words of my mouth, and the meditation of my heart, be acceptable in thy sight, O L*ORD*, my strength, and my redeemer.* (Ps. 19:12–14)

James recognized the deep spirituality of the Word and its inherent saving power in the following exhortation: *"Wherefore lay apart all filthiness and superfluity of naughtiness, and receive with meekness the engrafted word, which is able to save your souls"* (James 1:21).

And Peter talked along the same line when describing the saving power of the Word of God: *"Being born again, not of corruptible seed, but of incorruptible, by the word of God, which liveth and abideth for ever"* (1 Pet. 1:23). Not only did Peter speak of being born again by the incorruptible Word of God, but he informed us that to grow in grace we must be like

Prayer and Spiritual Warfare

newborn babes, desiring or feeding on the *"sincere milk of the word"* (1 Pet. 2:2).

Prayer invariably generates a love for the Word of God. Prayer leads people to obey the Word of God and puts an unspeakable joy into the obedient heart. Praying people and Bible-reading people are the same sort of folk. The God of the Bible and the God of prayer are one. God speaks to man in the Bible; man speaks to God in prayer. One reads the Bible to discover God's will. He prays in order to receive power to do that will. Bible reading and praying are the distinguishing traits of those who strive to know and please God.

Just as prayer generates a love for the Scriptures and causes people to begin to read the Bible, so prayer causes men and women to visit the house of God to hear the Scriptures expounded. Churchgoing is closely connected with the Bible, primarily because the Bible cautions us against *"forsaking the assembling of ourselves together, as the manner of some is"* (Heb. 10:25). Churchgoing also results because God's chosen minister explains and enforces the Scriptures upon his hearers. Prayer germinates a resolve in those who practice it to not forsake the church.

Prayer generates a churchgoing conscience, a church-loving heart, and a church-supporting spirit. Praying people take delight in the preaching of the Word and the support of the church. Prayer exalts the Word of God and gives it preeminence in those who faithfully and wholeheartedly call upon the name of the Lord.

Prayer draws its very life from the Bible. It places its security on the firm ground of Scripture. Its very existence and character depend on revelation made by God to man in His holy Word. Prayer, in turn, exalts this same revelation and turns men toward that Word. The nature, necessity, and all-comprehending character of prayer are based on the Word of God.

Psalm 119 is a directory of God's Word. With three or four exceptions, each verse contains a word that identifies or locates the Word of God. Quite often, the author broke out into supplication, several times praying, *"Teach me thy statutes"* (Ps. 119:12). He was so deeply impressed with the wonders of God's Word and with the need for divine illumination to see and understand the wonderful things recorded within that he fervently prayed, *"Open thou mine eyes, that I may behold wondrous things out of thy law"* (Ps. 119:18).

From the opening of this wonderful psalm to its close, prayer and God's Word are intertwined. Almost every phase of God's Word is touched on by this inspired writer. The psalmist was so thoroughly convinced of the deep spiritual power of the Word of God that he made this declaration: *"Thy word have I hid in mine heart, that I might not sin against thee"* (v. 11).

Here the psalmist found his protection against sinning. By having God's Word hidden in his heart and his whole being thoroughly impregnated with that Word, he was able to walk to and fro on the earth. He was safe from the attack of the enemy and strengthened from wandering away.

We find, furthermore, that the power of prayer creates a real love for the Scriptures and puts within men a nature that will take pleasure in the Word. In holy ecstasy the psalmist cried, *"O how I love thy law! it is my meditation all the day"* (v. 97). And again: *"How sweet are thy words unto my taste! yea, sweeter than honey to my mouth!"* (v. 103).

Do we relish God's Word? If so, then let us give ourselves continually to prayer. He who would have a heart for the reading of the Bible must not—dare not—forget to pray. A man who loves the Bible will also love to pray. A man who loves to pray will delight in the law of the Lord.

Our Lord was a man of prayer. He magnified the Word of God and often quoted the Scriptures. Right through His earthly life, Jesus observed Sabbath-keeping, churchgoing, and the reading of the Word of God. His prayer intermingled with them all: *"And he came to Nazareth, where he had been brought up: and, as his custom was, he went into the synagogue on the sabbath day, and stood up for to read"* (Luke 4:16).

Let it be said that no two things are more essential to a Spirit-filled life than Bible reading and secret prayer. They will help you to grow in grace, to obtain joy from living a Christian life, and to be established in the way of eternal peace. To neglect these all-important duties means leanness of soul, loss of joy, absence of peace, dryness of spirit, and decay in all that pertains to spiritual life. Neglecting these things paves the way for apostasy and gives the enemy an advantage such as he is not likely to ignore.

Reading God's Word regularly and praying habitually in the secret place of the Most High puts one where he is absolutely safe from the attacks of the enemy of souls. It guarantees him salvation and final victory through the overcoming power of the Lamb.

14
Prayer and the House of God

And dear to me the loud "Amen,"
Which echoes through the blest abode—
Which swells, and sinks, then swells again,
Dies on the walls—but lives with God!

Prayer affects places, times, occasions, and circumstances. It has to do with God and with everything that is related to God. It has an intimate and special relationship to His house. A church should be a sacred place, set apart from all unhallowed and secular uses, for the worship of God. As worship is prayer, the house of God is a place set apart for worship. It is no common place. It is where God dwells, where He meets with His people, and where He delights in the worship of His saints.

Prayer is always proper in the house of God. When prayer is a stranger there, it ceases to be God's house at all. Our Lord put particular emphasis on what the church is to be when He cast out the buyers and sellers in the temple. He repeated the words from Isaiah: *"It is written, My house shall be called the house of prayer"* (Matt. 21:13). He makes prayer preeminent above all else in the house of God. Those who sidetrack prayer or seek to minimize it pervert the church

119

of God and make it something less than it is ordained to be.

Prayer is perfectly at home in the house of God. It is no stranger, no mere guest; it belongs there. It has a peculiar affinity for the place. It has a divine appointment to be there.

The inner chamber is a sacred place for personal worship. The house of God is a holy place for united worship. The prayer closet is for individual prayer. The house of God is for mutual, united prayer. Yet, even in the house of God, there is the element of private worship. God's people are to worship Him and pray to Him, personally, even in public worship. The church is for the united prayer of kindred, yet individual, believers.

The life, power, and glory of the church is prayer. The life of its members is dependent on prayer. The presence of God is secured and retained by prayer. The very place is made sacred by its ministry. Without it, the church is lifeless and powerless. Without it, even the building itself is nothing more than any other structure. Prayer converts even the bricks, mortar, and lumber into a sanctuary, a Holy of Holies, where the Shekinah dwells. Prayer separates it, in spirit and in purpose, from all other buildings. Prayer gives a peculiar sacredness to the building, sanctifies it, sets it apart for God, and conserves it from all common and mundane affairs.

With prayer, the house of God becomes a divine sanctuary. So the tabernacle, moving about from place to place, became the Holy of Holies, because God and prayer were there. Without prayer, the building may be costly, perfect in its structure, attractive to the eye, but it comes down to the human, with nothing divine in it, and is on a level with all other buildings.

Prayer and the House of God

Without prayer, a church is like a body without spirit; it is a dead, inanimate thing. A church with prayer in it has God in it. When prayer is set aside, God is outlawed. When prayer becomes an unfamiliar exercise, then God Himself is a stranger there.

As God's house is a house of prayer, the divine intention is that people should leave their homes and go to meet Him in His own house. The building is set apart for prayer. God has made a special promise to meet His people there. It is their duty to go there for that specific end. Prayer should be the chief attraction for all spiritually-minded churchgoers. While it is conceded that the preaching of the Word has an important place in the house of God, prayer is its predominant, distinguishing feature. Not that all other places are sinful or evil in themselves or in their uses—they are secular and human, having no special conception of God in them.

The church is, essentially, spiritual and divine. The work belonging to other places is done without special reference to God. He is not specifically recognized or called upon. In the church, however, God is acknowledged, and nothing is done without Him. Prayer is the one distinguishing mark of the house of God. As prayer distinguishes the Christian from unsaved people, so prayer distinguishes God's house from all other houses. It is a place where faithful believers meet with their Lord.

As God's house is a house of prayer, prayer should enter into and underlie everything that is done there. Prayer belongs to every sort of work relating to the church. As God's house is a house where the business of praying is carried on, so is it a place where the business of making praying people out of prayerless people is done. The house of God is a divine workshop, and there the work of prayer goes on; or the house of God is a divine schoolhouse, in which the lesson of prayer is taught, where men and women learn to pray, and where they graduate from the school of prayer.

Any church that calls itself the house of God but fails to magnify and teach the great lesson of prayer should change its teaching to conform to the divine prayer pattern, or it should change the name of its building to something other than a church.

On an earlier page, I referred to the finding of the Book of the Law that was given to Moses from the Lord. How long that book had been there, we do not know. But when tidings of its discovery were carried to Josiah, he tore his clothes and was greatly disturbed. He lamented the neglect of God's Word and saw, as a natural result, the iniquity that abounded throughout the land.

And then, Josiah thought of God and commanded Hilkiah, the priest, to go and make inquiry of the Lord. Such neglect of the word of the law was too serious a matter to be treated lightly. God must be sought. Josiah and his nation needed to repent.

> *Go ye, inquire of the Lord for me, and for the people, and for all Judah, concerning the words of this book that is found: for great is the wrath of the Lord that is kindled against us, because our fathers have not hearkened unto the words of this book, to do according unto all that which is written concerning us.*
>
> (2 Kings 22:13)

However, that was not all. Josiah was bent on promoting a revival of religion in his kingdom. He gathered all the elders of Jerusalem and Judah together for that purpose. When they had come together, the king went into the house of the Lord and read all the words of the Book of the Covenant that was found in the house of the Lord.

With this righteous king, God's Word was of great importance. He esteemed it at its proper worth. He counted it to be of grave importance and consulted God in prayer about it. He gathered together the dignitaries of his kingdom, so that they, together with himself, could be instructed out of God's Book concerning God's law.

When Ezra was seeking the reconstruction of his nation, the people assembled themselves together as one man before the water gate.

> *And they spake unto Ezra the scribe to bring the book of the law of Moses, which the LORD had commanded to Israel. And Ezra the priest brought the law before the congregation both of men and women, and all that could hear with understanding….And he read therein before the street that was before the water gate from the morning until midday…and the ears of all the people were attentive unto the book of the law.*
> (Neh. 8:1–3)

This was Bible-reading day in Judah—a real revival of Scripture study. The leaders read the Law before the people. Their ears were keen to hear what God had to say to them out of the Book of the Law. But it was not only a Bible-reading day. It was a time when real preaching was done, as the following passage indicates: *"So they read in the book in the law of God distinctly, and gave the sense, and caused them to understand the reading"* (Neh. 8:8).

Here is the scriptural definition of preaching. No better definition can be given. To read the Word of

God distinctly, so that the people could hear and understand the words presented boldly and clearly—that was the method followed in Jerusalem on this auspicious day. The sense of the words was made clear in the meeting held before the water gate. The people were treated to a high type of expository preaching. That was true preaching—preaching of a sort that is sorely needed today so that God's Word may have the same effect on the hearts of the people. This meeting in Jerusalem surely contains a lesson that all present-day preachers should learn and heed.

No one, having any knowledge of the existing facts, will deny the comparative lack of expository preaching in the pulpit today, and no one should do other than lament the lack. Topical, controversial, and historical preaching have, one supposes, their rightful place. But expository preaching, the prayerful expounding of the Word of God, is preaching that *is* preaching—pulpit effort *par excellence.*

For its successful accomplishment, however, a preacher must be a man of prayer. For every hour spent in study, he will have to spend two on his knees. For every hour devoted to wrestling with an obscure passage of Holy Scripture, he must have two hours in which he is found wrestling with God. Prayer and preaching! Preaching and prayer! They cannot be separated. The ancient cry was, *"To your tents, O Israel!"* (1 Kings 12:16). The modern cry should be, "To your knees, O preachers, to your knees!"

About the Author

E dward McKendree Bounds was born on August 15, 1835, in a small, northeastern Missouri town. He attended a one-room school in Shelbyville, where his father served as a county clerk, and he was admitted to the bar shortly before he reached the age of nineteen. An avid reader of the Scriptures and an ardent admirer of John Wesley's sermons, Bounds practiced law until the age of twenty-four, when he suddenly felt called to preach the Gospel.

His first pastorate was in the nearby town of Monticello, Missouri. Yet, in 1861, while he was pastor of a Methodist Episcopal church in Brunswick, the Civil War began, and Bounds was arrested by Union troops and charged for sympathizing with the Confederacy. He was made a prisoner of war and was held for a year and a half before being transferred to Memphis, Tennessee, and finally securing his release.

Armed only with an unquenchable desire to serve God, Bounds traveled nearly one hundred miles on foot to join General Pierce's command in Mississippi. Soon afterward he was made chaplain to the Confederate troops in Missouri. After the defeat of General John Hood's troops at Nashville, Tennessee, Bounds was again among those who were captured and held until swearing loyalty to the United States.

Prayer and Spiritual Warfare

After the war, Bounds pastored churches in Nashville, Tennessee; Selma, Alabama; and St. Louis, Missouri. It was in Selma that he met Emma Barnett, whom he later married in 1876, and with whom he had three children, one of whom died at the age of six. After Emma's death, in 1887, Bounds married Emma's cousin, Harriet Barnett, who survived him. The family included their five children, as well as two daughters from his first marriage.

While he was in St. Louis, Bounds accepted a position as associate editor for the regional Methodist journal, the *St. Louis Advocate.* Then, after only nineteen months, he moved to Nashville to become the editor of the *Christian Advocate,* the weekly paper for the entire Methodist Episcopal denomination in the South.

The final seventeen years of his life were spent with his family in Washington, Georgia, where both Emma and Harriet had grown up. Most of the time he spent reading, writing, and praying, but he often took an active part in revival ministry. Bounds was also in the habit of rising at four o'clock each morning in order to pray to God, for the great cares of the world were always upon his heart. He died on August 24, 1913, still relatively unknown to most of the Christian sphere.

Since the time of the apostles, no man besides Edward McKendree Bounds has left such a rich inheritance of research into the life of prayer. Prayer was as natural to him as breathing the air. He made prayer first and foremost in his life because he knew it as the strongest link between man and God. In the time of E. M. Bounds, human weakness, through prayer, could access the power of the overcoming Son of God, Jesus Christ. The same is true to this day.

"And call upon me in the day of trouble:
I will deliver thee."
—Psalm 50:15

E.M. BOUNDS

The Weapon of Prayer
E. M. Bounds

What is more important than ministry? Prayer!
As E. M. Bounds explains God's need for people
who pray, he includes sketches of the prayer lives
of such dedicated Christians as David Brainerd,
George Müller, and Jonathan Edwards. Learn how
you can prepare yourself for effective participation
in the highest calling Christ has given the church—to
advance God's kingdom through prayer.

ISBN: 0-88368-457-8 • Pocket • 192 pages

WHITAKER
HOUSE

proclaiming the power of the Gospel through the written word
visit our website at www.whitakerhouse.com

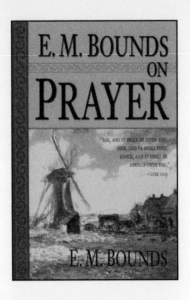

E. M. Bounds on Prayer
E. M. Bounds

Prayer is the Christian's lifeline to God, and with it lives
are changed for eternity! E. M. Bounds knew the secrets
of prayer and God's principles for supplying all our needs.
Here are his most cherished teachings on the life of prayer,
which is the only effective barrier against the powers of
evil so prevalent in this present world. Discover how
prayer can become your spiritual lifeline.

ISBN: 0-88368-416-0 • Trade • 624 pages

u
WHITAKER
HOUSE

proclaiming the power of the Gospel through the written word
visit our website at www.whitakerhouse.com